Language and the Teacher:
A Series in Applied Linguistics

Volume 13

under the editorial direction of

DR. ROBERT C. LUGTON

American Language Institute of New York University

LANGUAGE AND THE TEACHER:
A SERIES IN APPLIED LINGUISTICS

The series will be concerned with the following areas—

GENERAL STUDIES
Psycholinguistics, sociolinguistics, bilingualism.

GRAMMAR
Morphology, syntax, contrastive structure.

PHONOLOGY
Phonemics, intonation, contrastive phonetics, etc.

VOCABULARY STUDIES
Frequency counts, production and principles, lexicology.

READING SKILLS
Beginning skills, development, construction of texts,
literary reading.

WRITING SKILLS
Beginning skills, development, composition.

METHODOLOGY
Evaluation of methods, techniques, classroom practices.

**LANGUAGE TEACHING
FOR DIFFERENT AGE GROUPS**
Elementary, secondary, college, adult.

MACHINE TEACHING
Programmed learning, audio-visual equipment and
software, language laboratory.

TEACHER EDUCATION
Standards and evaluation, projects, curricula for
teacher training

ADMINISTRATION
Curriculum development, articulation, public relations.

TESTING
Techniques, statistical studies.

BIOGRAPHY

BIBLIOGRAPHY

ENGLISH AS A SECOND LANGUAGE

**METHODS OF RESEARCH IN LINGUISTICS
AND LANGUAGE TEACHING**

Language and the Teacher:
A Series in Applied Linguistics

Individualization of Instruction in Foreign Languages: A Practical Guide

Edited by

Ronald L. Gougher

Associate Professor of German
West Chester State College

THE CENTER FOR CURRICULUM DEVELOPMENT, INC.

401 Walnut Street   Philadelphia, Pa.

#2793

If a man does not keep pace with his companions, perhaps
it is because he hears a different drummer!
    —Henry David Thoreau

MARSHA and ROBERT

Table of Contents

I. Introduction

No longer can the foreign-language teaching profession rely on what this writer calls externals to *provide* an atmosphere in which it can comfortably pursue its linguistic and cultural goals. Externals, such as the pressure of Sputnik and its implications are gone, and with them, many of the philosophical and political tools to lobby for such funds as were provided in NDEA and EDPA programs, which were the boons of the 1960's for foreign-language education. Language requirements are under serious attack. Students demand more individual attention, more voice in the decision-making processes, and, in the eyes of many, make a lot of sense when they question the goals and results of foreign-language programs in America.

As a result, the profession is taking more and more time to look at itself in an attempt to re-evaluate old reasoning and formulate new aesthetic and practical goals for American students and teachers involved in foreign-language education. Indeed, the profession senses troubled times!

As other human beings in times of turmoil, many of the members of the language-teaching profession are seeking, some *groping* for, safe ground on which they might stand—certainly safer footing than the immediate future seems to promise, given the same learning-teaching conditions that have prevailed in American language teaching for the past twenty years or more. Knowing that they must defend their discipline now more than they have had to in the recent past, the majority of teachers of foreign language seek more exciting, attractive programs to stimulate student interest and performance. They seek more professional security also! Most, in fact, want to know *how* to develop a good educational rationale in which sound practice and credible linguistic and cultural goals are stressed so that they *can* defend their discipline when called upon to do so.

One answer, although not a panacea, seems to be individualization of instruction and learning, emphasizing performance objectives according to the optimum rates and interests of individual students. Individualization has become increasingly attractive, as its theory and practice are headlined in schools, in-service institutes, conferences, in the entire Volume 2 of *The Britannica Review of Foreign Language Education,* and at a recent blue-ribbon national gathering on the topic at Stanford University. Although theory has definitely begun to blossom, practice lags *awesomely!*

What, then, is the prognosis for successful practice on a large-scale basis in the near future? Perhaps a combination of professional insecurity, concerned students, parents, teachers, and administrators, and an idea whose time has come will provide for more effective, meaningful foreign-language learning in America—not tomorrow or the next day, to be sure: there is a lot of work to be done. A truly effective method of instruction on an individual basis for *all* students is a few years off, but it will come! We, as a profession, must start on small-scale programs, producing good results as we proceed, increasing quantity as quality develops, quality for all students at specified levels of performance; however, it seems that the beginnings will, indeed, be modest. Let us have modest successes with individualization and not gigantic failures.

During the past six years this writer has endeavored to put individualized instruction into practice in both public and private secondary schools and colleges. He has edited a newsletter, *Individualization of Foreign Language Learning in America,* has begun work on curriculum to facilitate individualized instruction, has lectured throughout the United States on the topic, and is writing one chapter on individualization for *The Britannica Review of Foreign Language Education, Volume 3.* While engaged in all these activities, he has heard one question most often—*How do we do it under present circumstances?* So it seems fitting to present to the profession at least one concise, practical guide now, knowing full well that more ambitious efforts will follow in the not-too-distant future.

Let this small treatise and the bibliography be just that—a guide, a motivator, an aid, *not* a New Deal in education.

Ronald L. Gougher

II. Defining Individualized Instruction of Foreign Languages

Mr. Gougher is a specialist in the teaching of German and individualized instruction. He has taught German on both secondary and university levels. In 1965 he was cited by the Pennsylvania State Superintendent of Public Instruction for "Distinguished Contribution to the Advancement of Education." Mr. Gougher has presented lectures on individualization to professional groups over the past five years, and is a consultant in this field for secondary schools and colleges. At present, Mr. Gougher is Associate Professor of German at West Chester State College in Pennsylvania.

It seems to be senseless for any teacher to think about *starting* to individualize foreign-language instruction on a formal basis before he arrives at some sort of practical definition as it might apply to his school. Without being able to explicate the idea as it fits his own situation, the teacher turns out to be a poor proponent, indeed, a very weak salesman.

Just how is individualization defined with reference to foreign-language study? What does it mean for the student and teacher of foreign languages? The guidelines suggested here should provide ideas to help each teacher answer the question for himself.

Note from the outset that this writer is *not* trying to establish a dogmatic definition for individualization; he *is* suggesting basic understandings toward the *development* of definitions, first by presenting underlying premises and then specific guidelines.

Teachers must not make the mistake of confusing individualized instruction with independent study, although it is true that independent study might well be an integral part of an individualized program. Instruction does imply some effort on the teacher's part beyond pointing a finger toward a pile of books and tapes and saying, "Go forth and pursue knowledge!" It goes far beyond having students merely *do* things by themselves without proper human guidance. Eyeball-to-eyeball education is an important matter in an individualized program – a teacher should be espousing an educational philosophy based on helping and dealing with people.

Individualized instruction must include some sort of preconceived pattern of activities on the part of the teacher related to his students, allowing for their individual differences in ability, interest, and motivation. A teacher acts as a guide to, planning assistant for, and periodical evaluator of students on a one-to-one or small-group basis.

Specifically, in foreign-language instruction, the teacher must be concerned with performance of skills more than in other areas of the humanities, and that fact produces some uniqueness in definition. The uniqueness in definition is caused by specific learning activities, especially at the beginning levels of study. Individualized instruction in foreign languages implies some method of facilitating the acquisition of *skills* at each student's own optimum rate. In the very beginning of and throughout an entire individualized foreign-language program, the emphasis is placed on *learning* the language skills and *learning about* the language-related cultural areas, not on *teaching*. Indeed, it is questionable whether we really do *teach* a language! A good *teacher* in an individualized foreign-language program corrects errors, supplies acceptable models for skill performance, and *guides* each student in his individual learning activity. He prescribes as little as possible; he *provides* an opportunity for the student to learn.

Some specific guidelines for defining individualized instruction have been gleaned from the author's own practice and from those experiments he has observed and studied. A combination of the basic understandings presented and these guidelines should serve as a reasonable basis for each teacher to develop a definition of individualized instruction in foreign languages as it applies practically in his local school setting.

1. Ideally, each student should be allowed to progress at his own optimum rate. Remember, it might just be practical and efficient in foreign-language instruction to guide some of the students in *small groups* to facilitate learning at an optimum rate for each person involved. Since some students may well achieve certain performance objectives in the foreign language best in groups of as many as ten or fifteen, the teacher is still

individualizing for those students, as he provides the opportunity for learning the language skills in an efficient, practical manner. But the group method is not good for solving all the educational problems involved in foreign-language study. The teacher must decide when to work in groups, when to work on a one-to-one basis. With well-conceived curricular materials and proper teacher-student orientation, one-to-one and mini-group methods can complement each other.

2. Students should be tested *often* for performance, preferably when they want to be tested. They must know what they are to know, when, and why. The "what, when, and why" are decided in joint planning between student and teacher. Tests are not used *simply* to assign grades, but more importantly, to find out what the student has not learned. When a student has helped to plan a testing date and does not perform as he should, he has learned something about his own planning ability, as well as having discovered he did not acquire necessary skills to be able to proceed. It is the teacher's responsibility to provide the student with an opportunity to attain those objectives. Until a student achieves the performance objectives for each unit or packet assigned, he does not go on. Obviously, there are practical limitations.

3. When *evaluating* a student for performance, a teacher might accept 80% accuracy, allowing the student to proceed, while working for increased accuracy in the future. If the student moves ahead only after achieving 80% accuracy, he does not receive less than a "B" in any foreign-language course, although he may use more time to earn the grade than other students. It thus becomes far less necessary to pass students with "C" and "D" grades in foreign-language study. A revised system of credit, to be explained later, will assist the teacher in objective grading of student performance.

4. In the absence of any real consensus about what levels mean, what constitutes one, two, or three credits, and so forth, each school must determine what performance objectives are necessary for each level. Hopefully, each teacher will try seriously to define realistic, yet challenging objectives to be performed by each individual student at each level. Then, too, it is not too idealistic to hope for professionals to define well what levels mean and, in so doing, help the *teacher* to define those elusive limits. It would make individualization a bit easier for all.

5. Although each student should be given an opportunity to move at as near his own optimum rate as possible, since some *common* goals and performance objectives are necessary, so too are some limitations *unavoidable*. Although some say failure can be eliminated, this writer can not agree. With more individualization, percentages of failure decrease; however, in the vast majority of schools failure will still occur, even if herculean pedagogical tasks are performed by the nation's cadre of foreign-language teachers.

6. A teacher or teacher aid might act as a guide when the student or small group of students needs assistance, i.e., when the student is confused about suggested performance objectives in the target language or about his own curriculum planning and goal setting. The student needs help, too, when he ceases to perform at his own optimum rate, as well as when his interest and motivation wane. The teacher acts as a catalyst toward further progress.

7. Each student should help to plan his own curriculum. He must understand the nature of his learning tasks and know how he is expected to change his language skills. He must know exactly what he is to learn and with what proficiency. It is extremely important that each student match what he thinks he can do with what he actually does.

8. Economic disaster would be forecast by school leaders, if teachers were to announce that each student had to have his own unique set of materials! In most schools it is absolutely *necessary* to build a program around some established text, organizing specific learning aids and resource material about the core. Remember, it is quite possible that as many as half the students taught by one instructor might learn well an established set of performance objectives at the same rate and move on from that *point* on a more individual basis according to interest and ability.

At any given point, the rate of learning and certain interest areas might suit a small group, while enrichment materials, properly arranged, will help other students move ahead faster, mastering *both the common and additional material* well. Still others will spend more time on remedial work to achieve proficiency levels at acceptable performance limits.

9. The idea that one year's study should equal one credit must be discarded. Obviously, some method for defining a proficiency level must be devised, and the student must be given the neces-

sary time to achieve it. It is definitely true that many students can achieve performance objectives in the target language at the rate of about one level per year; however, about fifteen to twenty percent of the students involved in most foreign-language programs could earn more than one proficiency level in one year, if they were given the opportunity. Somewhat fewer would benefit from programs in which they were allowed to take more time to learn language skills equivalent to fewer levels better.

10. Awarding of credit must be highly individualized. Established credit might be awarded to each student when he can produce those performance objectives prescribed in advance as necessary level limits, that is, the performance level below which no full credit may be awarded. Why not reduce credit to ½ or ¼ units to provide a sense of achievement at an earlier point in time for those who can learn language faster, and, at the same time, provide a credit level limit that divides one proficiency level into more readily attainable goals for the slower student? Both the faster and the slower learner receive credit for a job well done.

11. Credit need not be awarded to each student, one at a time. The teacher must judge when many students should be evaluated at one time with credit granted, as well as when small groups and individuals have to be evaluated and accredited on one-to-one bases.

12. If the school does not provide flexible scheduling, then the teacher must inject flexibility into his own schedule. The chapter in which experimental programs are discussed will provide some helpful hints toward manipulation of time.

In practice, there can be no one definition for individualized instruction in foreign-language study. This writer encourages the reader to think about the foregoing suggestions and formulate his own definition. Then apply it! Practical hints in subsequent chapters should help the teacher in his task of orienting himself to the philosophy of individualization and to the difficult job of application in the real school setting.

III. The State of Individualized Foreign- Language Instruction in 1970

In this short survey, the author will present a brief overview of individualized foreign-language instruction as it stands at the beginning of the decade. Included will be both theory and practice, what has been written and what is being done.

Probably the most inclusive volume to date on all aspects of individualized foreign-language instruction is the *Britannica Review of Foreign Language Education, Volume II.* When a prestigious organization such as the American Council for the Teaching of Foreign Languages chooses to support such a project, the profession must presume that there is a real need for taking a good look at individualized instruction as it applies to foreign-language learning. In *BRFLE, II,* there are excellent reviews and evaluations of the specific elements about which foreign-language teachers must begin to concern themselves. One finds a well-developed rationale for individualized instruction and also scholarly, yet practical discussions of behavioral objectives, curriculum development, educational media, language laboratories, and teacher training as each aspect applies to individualized foreign-language instruction.

Growing interest in both theory and practice of individualized foreign-language instruction is easily documented as the decade begins. *Individualization of Foreign Language Learning in America,* a newsletter devoted to disseminating information about individualized instruction, printed and distributed by the Foreign Language Department of West Chester State College, Pennsylvania, has been received and publicized widely by most of the major national and state foreign-language journals.[1] An informative column has been dedicated to individualized instruction in *Foreign Language Annals.*

Foreign-language conferences have been devoting more and more time and effort to explicating individualized instruction and providing helpful insights about programs in practice. A major conference on individualized foreign-language instruction was held at Stanford University in May of 1971, and reports of the conference are probably available as this book appears in print.

Although there have existed in the past many opportunities for individualized learning, e.g., the tutorial, independent study, and individual attention given to the student in the one-room schoolhouse, there appears now to be a new interest in and thrust given to individualized learning due to the desire on the part of many students for more self-identity, self-orientation, and self-direction. Many students seem to want opportunities to prepare for the future in an innovative American society.

With the change in educational processes toward individualized instruction has come a gradual change in the roles of the teacher, the administrator, and the student. The teacher, traditionally a dispenser of knowledge and center of the learning process, is gradually becoming more of a guide, a planner of performance objectives, a counselor, a diagnostician, and an evaluator. Administrators are becoming more involved in allowing time for teachers to prepare materials for individualized instruction. There is a developing trend on the part of administrators to support innovations toward individualization. The "new" student is facing more tasks himself and becoming more responsible for learning about his own strengths and weaknesses. He needs the opportunity to do so, and many teachers recognize it and are beginning to act accordingly.

Defining individualized instruction is providing a perplexing problem for educators, as witnessed in an ever-increasing number of articles aimed at defining exactly what it is the profession is trying to do for the contemporary foreign-language student. The bibliography provided in the last section of this guide provides information necessary for each teacher to arrive at his own definition for his own school.

Programs in practice have developed in various formats, the

---

[1] *Individualization of Foreign Language Learning in America* is edited by John F. Bockman and Ronald L. Gougher and is available upon request at West Chester State College, Pennsylvania.

most popular being some variety of self-pacing with emphasis on performance objectives and not on time spent or exposure to language study. Other areas being investigated by many foreign-language teachers to facilitate implementation of individualized programs are:

1. Programmed Learning
2. Small Group Instruction
3. Mini-courses
4. Individually Prescribed Instruction
5. Independent Study
6. Computer-Assisted Instruction
7. Differentiated Staffing

There are programs in practice representing all areas at all educational levels, most of them in pilot, experimental programs.[2]

The fervor over individualized instruction has caused educators to look to the past for older ideas and to relate them to the "new" trends. Indeed, there is much borrowed, some things old and some things new emerging in theory and practice.

Admittedly, the vast majority of programs in practice are still small. "Full-scale" programs stand in the extreme minority.

In the future, many teachers will be asked to individualize foreign-language programs. Thoughtful contemplation and careful planning will be necessary to avoid educational disasters in the name of individualized foreign-language learning. At the core of it all will stand the teacher, and one of the most important trends will be toward training him to operate successfully in the educational processes involved in individualized foreign-language learning.

---

[2] See Ronald L. Gougher, "Individualization of Foreign Language Learning: What is Being Done," in Dale L. Lange, *Britannica Review of Foreign Language Education, Volume III*, Chicago, 1971.

IV. The Foreign-Language Teacher and the Process of Change: A Case for Individualized Instruction

Dr. Otto has taught Spanish at the secondary and university levels and has published numerous articles related to foreign-language education. He received the Stephen A. Freeman award for the most outstanding article submitted to a professional foreign-language journal during the 1968–1970 period.

INTRODUCTION

Dr. Frank Otto, Professor of Foreign-Language Education at the Ohio State University, offers insight into the processes of educational change at the start of the decade. His experience in foreign-language education at all educational levels equips him well to guide teachers in beginning efforts toward indivualized programs. The short outline for teacher-administrator workshops in individualization should prove helpful to those intent on educational change toward individualized instruction in foreign languages.

Today, in our type of culture, both adults and children live in a world most acutely aware of the reality of change as a permanent element in human life. In the light of this awareness, one may wonder what "education" really means. Education might best be thought of as a process of exposure and meaningful experiences rather than a concern chiefly with fostering the acquisition of any given amount of facts to be "learned." In its more innovative trends, it concerns itself primarily with helping the growth, intellectual and otherwise, of the individual student engaged in the process of learning.

9

A REVIEW OF TRENDS IN EDUCATION

There is developing in our society a desire to look at man, his world, his society, and his institutions which serve society's needs, from new perspectives. The development of technology that has freed man so that he can encounter the world more creatively and less passively, the growing desire of man to reflect on himself and to perceive his world from his own viewpoint as well as through the eyes of others, and the movement that is suggesting alternative ways to conceptualize the experience of education, all lead to a new central theme and concept—"individualizing instruction."

Ivan Illich presents education with one of the most striking alternatives to institutionalized public instruction when he suggests that society de-school itself by eliminating compulsory education, issuing edu-credit cards to all at birth to be used as desired throughout one's life, and guaranteeing no monopoly of education by public agencies. Such a change would virtually assure the possibility of the development of alternatives in educational experiences, for education would become a consumer's market as much as the consumer would desire. If this plan were to be implemented, the changes within the educational system would be traumatic; however, the fact that change must occur in this direction seems supportable when one examines the nature of some of the alternative programs actually in operation today. Storefront centers, street academies, the Job Corps, and VISTA all promote educational experiences through "media" other than the traditional schoolhouse. These programs serve as testimony to the fact that the challenge for alternatives must be responded to in some meaningful way. Philadelphia's Parkway Program, or "schools without walls," is another example of an innovative response to the challenge that we place educational experiences in perspective with other common experiences. While some of these programs may not survive in their present form, their very presence today has proved the viability of the belief that alternatives to what we have must be developed and can be implemented in an effort to individualize instruction. If nothing else, they will serve as a not-so-subtle pressure on the educational system to change. As John Fischer has recently observed, almost everyone associated in some way with the American educational system is dissatisfied with present performance. This charge does not necessarily imply that education needs to go non-public as a solution. The implication is that these functioning alternatives will encourage the needed thorough examination of present practices and their underlying assumptions in more profitable directions than dissatisfaction alone may permit.

Compensatory lock-step instructional programs have failed because they have only served to imprison more people more completely into a system of educational experience that, by its very nature, forces everyone to run the same race and play the same game; in such a case, failure is inevitable because the definition of acceptable success is built right in. We are now charged with the task of providing as many games or races as the people wish to run, or better, of ridding ourselves of the notions of "game" and "race." It is only within this context that failure in all of its manifestations, but most importantly in the educational setting, can be removed. Otherwise, we will be saddled with the concept of failure[1] and the realization that the system itself has failed in its responsibility of responding to the needs of all in society who request services of it. Such a system cannot survive because it will not be permitted to survive.

THE CONCEPT OF CHANGE AS IT RELATES TO FOREIGN LANGUAGE PROGRAMS

If the teacher's role is to induce learning, help the child find the learning style best suited to his personality and, generally speaking, help him learn how to learn and become conscious of his learning; if the teacher is to be a "human teaching artist," then it may be that much of what goes on in our foreign-language classrooms is frightfully out of focus. We must seek answers to questions concerning:

1. The redefinition and diversification of our goals and objectives and changes in the methods and curricular patterns used to attain these goals.
2. The role of teacher and student in the process of teaching and learning for mastery. We need to explore the mutual relationship of the teacher and student as they evolve a program of mastery together.

---

[1] Traditionally, the concept of failure refers to a low level of student achievement. I propose that we begin looking at other indicators of failure, for certainly it is just as possible for a program to fail a student as it is for a student to "fail" a program. Student interest, sense of achievement and retention in the program must be considered as factors that are important to the growth of the foreign-language program.

3. The curriculum: course offerings and format; a consideration of effective ways of fitting foreign-language study into the general curriculum as an integral part of that curriculum.
4. Individualizing the student's environment and experiences.
5. The effective staffing and presentation of new programs in order to provide the most relevant and individualized learning situation for as many students as possible.

GENERAL OBJECTIVES

The first kind of objective to define is one which the whole profession might commit itself to as its ultimate goal: that second-language instruction should be an integral part of the basic education of every child. A clear commitment to this objective would be innovative in at least two ways: it would give the profession a goal of greater breadth than it has ever envisaged before, and it would place the responsibility for such programs with those who are to implement them and make them a day-to-day reality. The overall objective would be that of providing the most relevant and individualized learning situation for as many students as possible.

Curriculum, course content and format, teaching strategies, teacher's attitudes, even to a large extent student motivation, all depend on what goals teachers and students have set for themselves. In defining objectives, every element of the total situation where the teaching and the learning take place must be considered. National, social, individual factors all have a bearing on languages that will be studied, on the reasons for studying them, on how, how long, and for what purposes they will be studied.

SPECIFIC OBJECTIVES

DEVELOPING BASIC GOALS OF INSTRUCTION

Most teachers and teacher educators would agree that there is a basic core of material that should be presented and ultimately mastered by students as they progress along a continuum of foreign-language study. Perhaps it makes sense, then, to define each level of instruction at least in terms of desirable linguistic skills in the areas of phonology, morphology, and syntax. This objective is possible to achieve and must be considered of primary importance if we are to provide our foreign-language students with program continuity.

TEACHING AND LEARNING FOR MASTERY

The closer one gets to the practical tasks of teaching, the more imperative it becomes that we have a clear view of how teaching and learning for mastery can occur at various levels and with students of a wide range of competence. Student behavior must be defined in terms of carefully stated specifications of terminal performance or proficiency criteria.

The pacing of learning experience is crucial. Careful attention must be given to task analysis: first, what the student should be able to do to accomplish each of the performance objectives previously defined as a minimal step within levels of mastery and, second, what the teacher needs to do in order to lead the student to the accomplishment of each performance objective.

MODULAR SCHEDULING

In a traditional schedule, instruction time usually remains constant. Any approach that can create a better utilization of time is extremely valuable. Modular scheduling is an innovation which affects scope and sequence and seeks to individualize the teaching as well as the learning process. The primary objective of modular scheduling is to better utilize the curriculum, teacher and pupil input (time, talent and preparation) in order to achieve higher levels of program output (student competence, student motivation, and teacher and student satisfaction).

Program Input	*Program Output*
Foreign language and the curriculum (time)	Student competence
	Student motivation
Teachers (talent)	Teacher and student
Pupils (preparation)	satisfaction

Modular scheduling is used to obtain a more varied treatment of any one or all three of the basic inputs involved in the learning process (foreign language and the curriculum, the pupils, and the teachers).

The Subject and the Curriculum: Alternating among individual study, large-group, small-group, and programmed activities offers one of the most promising approaches to breaking the lockstep without prohibitively increasing the costs of instruction.

The Pupils: Since course-work in foreign languages is highly cumulative, it is difficult for some students to keep up with the group. These students could easily be recycled and have the opportunity to either begin again during the same academic year or go back for remedial work in an area of particular difficulty. Hopefully, attrition rates at various levels could be lowered significantly.

The Teachers: Modular scheduling offers definite possibilities for differentiating responsibilities among members of the foreign-language teaching staff. A team comprised of master teachers, staff teachers, para-professionals, non-certificated personnel, resource people and advanced foreign-language students can help implement a program that truly individualizes instruction.

Activities include:
   a) large-group instruction
   b) small-group instruction
   c) programmed (automated self-instructional, self-evaluating, and self-pacing activities)
   d) individual conferences with the teacher
   e) individual study
   f) unstructured time

INDIVIDUALIZED INSTRUCTION

Individual study provides a learning situation which allows a student to develop personal competencies through experiences as an individual but in interaction with others when needed. It is characterized by increasing personal responsibility and decreasing faculty supervision. It is in individual study that students have the opportunities to develop competencies in line with their own special interests and to the extent of their abilities. Schools need to provide individual pupils with opportunities to study and work apart from the mass in order for students to develop responsibility for their own learning. Every effort must be made to correlate topics and projects with the basic objectives of the foreign-language program.

Whenever a student's time is involved in individual study, responsibility is placed on the teacher to develop in the student the desire to master material and skills. It is the responsibility of the teacher to serve as a resource person, directing students into meaningful activities stressing reinforcement and practical application. It is the teacher's responsibility to establish a continuing contact with each student involved in individual study and to hold the student accountable for work in each phase of the program. Teachers constantly need to resist the temptation to compare and contrast the results of individual study among students. The goal is the individual development of each student according to his own pace, interests, and talents. The fundamental concern is student progress in terms of his own interests, potential, and development at a given stage, not a comparison of his progress in relation to other students in his group.

In the student role, the emphasis is on the individual's role in learning. This concept recognizes that all students possess the potential for self-initiative, self-discipline, and productivity. A student performing effectively in individual study is one who personalizes learning and strives for improvement. It is also the responsibility of each student involved in individual study to establish continuing contact with his teacher.

Individual study programs are student-centered in their goals. Mutually acceptable needs and goals become the criteria for planning and, even though there may appear to be too many variations (mini-courses), technology and grouping can be utilized to accommodate numerous variations economically and efficiently. The subject matter (phonology, morphology, syntax) will remain the nucleus, but the individual student's needs will dictate the approach to the subject matter. The pattern and quantity of learning activities will be in part suggested by the teacher in response to the problems and interests of each student.

DIFFERENTIATED STAFFING

It is readily apparent that one person cannot possibly assume full responsibility for all the tasks included in the successful implementation of a foreign-language program emphasizing teaching and learning for mastery through modular scheduling and/or the open classroom approach. There must be a division of tasks, authority, and commensurate responsibility.

There exist numerous definitions and models of differentiated staffing. Although there is a great deal of flexibility within these models, there are a few guidelines that may be considered if you are contemplating a plan for differentiating staff assignments:

1. Levels of competence and responsibility should be considered, but in terms of training and teacher proficiency rather than grade point average, transcript credit, or years of experience. Remunerations should be commensurate with the responsibilities outlined for each position designated on the staff model.

2. It is difficult to endorse a particular model for differentiating staff assignments since one of the basic concepts is that all teachers should be involved in planning the division of responsibilities in order that their role be in keeping with their interests, talents and abilities. All staff members should be included in a team approach to decision making and planning since their instructional tasks will be more directly affected than ever before. You may want to think in terms of three basic categories of personnel within a school system or school building: Professional, para-professional, and pre-service.

    a) The professional category usually includes a coordinator, master teachers, and staff teachers. Teachers in the professional category must be relieved of as many non-instructional and maintenance responsibilities as possible. Teacher aides, secretaries and language-lab technicians should be employed to address themselves to these tasks.

    b) The para-professional category includes the native informant, teacher aide, language-laboratory technician, and language secretary.

    c) The pre-service category includes student teachers, teaching interns, and advanced foreign-language students.

3. In a teaching situation where faculty assignments are differentiated according to training, ability and interests, lesson and unit planning become team endeavors with each staff member contributing his talents and efforts to meet a mutual challenge to individualize instruction.

4. The development, implementation, evaluation of the instructional program are the collective responsibility of the entire team. Because of the close-working relationships that develop among team members, and because of the critical importance attached to each task as part of a pattern, the staff must be involved in decision-making regarding the selection, retention, and assignment of their colleagues on the teaching team.

The contributions of each member of the instructional team must be carefully coordinated and blended into a meaningful program of learning activities. Each teacher must be free to choose learning activities that meet the needs of his students as well as his own capabilities and teaching style. As we all know, what goes on behind the closed classroom door is our prerogative. We tend to present material and activities in a manner compatible with our training, pedagogical beliefs, and interests.

IMPLICATIONS FOR TEACHER PREPARATION PROGRAMS

The teacher is no longer strictly the disseminator of information; in the future, students will have more access to information sources such as libraries, communications media, and computer memory banks than to their teachers. If there is to be change, it is to be a change in the role of the teacher from that of *the* source of information to that of a stimulus for learning and a guide to many sources of information.

Change is clearly needed. But change must be based on clearly-stated objectives rather than on random exploration with the rationale written after the fact. Teachers will need to be trained to be competent organizers and diagnosticians in order to provide the leadership needed to accomplish the long- and short-range goals described above. A part-whole relationship must be established so that each experience fits meaningfully into the day's, week's, or unit's sequence of instruction.

INNOVATIONS

1. The new role of the teacher and other support personnel.
2. The effective use of space and facilities.
3. The effective use of software such as the syllabus, course content and realia.
4. The impact of innovative foreign-language programs on student and teacher attitudes and motivation.
5. The expeditious use of professional laboratory experiences for prospective foreign-language teachers.

CONCLUSION

In order to approach a description of the trends becoming evident in foreign-language education, one could indicate in what way these trends will contribute to the development of the role of the foreign-language teacher as "an architect and manager of the learning process." While this is only one way in which these broad areas of concern could be approached, it would seem that it is the most productive way in terms of addressing oneself to the implications which would occur relevant to these changing roles of the teacher and the student—the context, after all, where learning is assumed to take place. There are three general areas in which change or pressure for change is occurring in the foreign-language education field: (1) the definition of goals and the establishment of curricular patterns designed to attain those goals; (2) the roles conceptualized for the teacher and the student in the process of working toward those goals; and (3) the way in which school facilities, personnel, structures and programs influence the operation and direction of the foreign-language program.

Once certain assumptions are made or accepted with regard to curricular goals and patterns, the role of the teacher or the student within that context is determined accordingly. It is becoming widely accepted that learning a foreign language to achieve a particular individual's set of educational objectives does not mean passing or failing him according to his achievement within a particular time interval given one set of materials according to a particular procedure, but rather permitting him and leading him to achieve mastery of the skills at hand. This would mean that all teaching and learning styles which can possibly be identified are valid if they serve to facilitate the achievement of mastery.

The facilities, personnel, broad curricular structures, and general program patterns of a school influence the operation of a foreign-language program in two ways. They influence the teaching of foreign languages directly by providing the context in which the foreign-language program has to work. Furthermore, they provide examples of how other programs in the curriculum are operating and indicate the range of possibilities open to the foreign-language program if it deems these desirable for its purposes.

The broad curricular patterns of the non-graded school and the modular schedule, which so frequently accompanies it, open up many avenues to the foreign-language teacher attempting to provide a set of educational experiences which will permit mastery by each individual according to his own objectives. Thus, the student in a school with modular scheduling could elect to spend more time in foreign-language work where he may need the time the most. In the non-graded setting, the teacher could monitor the student's progress so that he would move into a new phase of learning only after he has mastered the preceding phase.

The presence of para-professional and pre-service personnel in the school setting permits new roles to be defined for the classroom teacher. Freed from clerical and disciplinary functions, the foreign-language teacher can spend more time working individually with students and planning the kinds of foreign-

language experiences which will meet the needs of the individuals involved. Technologists and curriculum developers
also have contributed their efforts to facilitate the foreign-
language teacher's role in individualizing instruction. The
technologist can provide him with a variety of tools designed to
give students carefully controlled practice in given skill areas.
The curriculum specialist can provide him with information
about the overall picture of what is happening to the student as
he moves through his entire school day, for it is only with this
information that the foreign-language teacher can provide experiences that will support rather than contradict the broad
objectives defined by the school. Other professional personnel
in guidance and counseling can give the foreign-language
teacher much needed information about the particular individuals involved and their unique educational objectives so
that the foreign-language experience can become meaningful
to them.

Through the curriculum specialists, school administrator, and
his own efforts, the foreign-language teacher should become
thoroughly familiar with the other experiences encountered by
his students during the school day. It is perhaps only by recognizing the vast influence of these programs on his students'
learning styles and educational expectations that he may fully
realize the necessity for change in the foreign-language program.[2] Indeed, the task of meshing the foreign-language program
with the other parts of the curriculum might be the most difficult one faced by the foreign-language teacher today.

Considering the complexity of all these present trends and
their intricate interrelationships (for example, if one chooses to
use individualized instruction as his basic goal of educational
experiences, he will immediately see the applicability of
non-gradedness, flexible scheduling, differentiated staffing, and
programmed instruction as possible inputs leading to the attainment of this objective), one appreciates the aptness of calling the
foreign-language teacher an architect and manager of the learn-

---

[2] An example here might serve to make the cruciality of this point more
clear: if the physical sciences and the social sciences along with studies
in English as well, are increasingly emphasizing what might be called
concept learning, then the attempt of a foreign-language program to be
solely concerned with rote learning and skill development in a strict
stimulus-response pattern might be met with confusion and frustration
by the student.

ing process with reference to each individual learning experience. It might even be more appropriate to call him a humane teaching artist—with the talents of a magician—if he is indeed able to successfully meet the challenge of providing the most relevant and individualized learning situation for as many students as possible.

This article was written with the hope that teachers would meet the challenge to become involved in planning and implementing a foreign-language program that seeks to individualize instruction. For this reason, a list of selected readings is provided. In addition, a list of possible questions for discussion at in-service meetings and workshops has been included. With the cooperation of your administrators and/or foreign-language coordinator, it may be possible to consider the questions provided for discussion. If feasible, members of committees could seek solutions to these and other problems confronting foreign-language teachers who plan to develop individualized instructional programs.

SELECTED READINGS

Adams, Charles L. "Independence for Study," *Hispania*, L, 483–87.

Alexander, William M., and Hines, Vynce A. *Independent Study in Secondary Schools*. New York, Holt, Rinehart and Winston, Inc., 1967.

Archibeque, Joe D. "Utilizing the Advanced Student as a Classroom Tutor," *Hispania*, LIII, No. 1, March 1970, 70–2.

Arnspiger, Robert H. "All He Is Capable of Becoming," *School and Community*, November 1968.

Banathy, Bela H., Boris Jordan. "A Classroom Laboratory Instructional System (CLIS)" *Foreign Language Annals*, II, No. 4, May 1969, 466–473.

Banathy, Bela H. "The Systems Approach," *Modern Language Journal*, LI, 1967, 281–289.

Barrutia, Richard. "Computerized Foreign Language Instruction." *Hispania*, LIII, 3 (September 1970), 361–71.

Bishop, Lloyd K. "Computerized Modular Scheduling: A Technical Breakthrough for More Flexible School Programs," *Kappa Delta Pi Record*, October 1968, 17–19.

Brown, B. Frank. *The Non-Graded High School*. Englewood Cliffs, N.J., Prentice-Hall, 1963.

Bull, William E. "Task Analysis and Foreign Language Teaching," *The Florida Foreign Language Reporter*, 5, Winter 1966–67, 3–4.

Bush, Robert. "Redefining the Role of the Teacher," *Theory Into Practice*, VI, No. 5, Dec. 1967, 246–251.

Carroll, John B. "A Model for Research in Programmed Self-Instruction," In G. Mathieu, ed. *Advances in the Teaching of Modern Languages*. Pergamon Press, 1966, 11–46.

Ciotti, Marianne C. "A Conceptual Framework for Small-Group Instruction in High School," *Foreign Language Annals*, I, October 1969, 75–89.

Continuous Progress Foreign Language Program. P. L. 89–10. Title III project submitted by the West Bend Public Schools, Joint District No. 1, West Bend, Wisconsin, 1967.

Crosby, Muriel. "Who Changes the Curriculum and How?" *Phi Delta Kappan*, LI, No. 7, March 1970, 385–389.

Doll, Ronald C. "The Multiple Forces Affecting Curriculum Change," *Phi Delta Kappan*, LI, No. 7, March 1970, 382–384.

Edelfelt, Roy A.; Allen, Dwight W.; et al, "Staff Differentiation and the Preparation of Educational Personnel," *Yearbook of the American Association of Colleges for Teacher Education*. 1968, Washington, D.C.

Engler, David. "Instructional Technology and the Curriculum," *Phi Delta Kappan*, LI, No. 7, March 1970, 379–82.

English, Fenwick, "Questions and Answers on Differentiated Staffing," *Today's Education* 58:53–54, March, 1969.

Estarellas, Juan. "The Self-Instructional Foreign Language Program at Florida Atlantic University." *Hispania*, LIII, 3 (September 1970), 371–85.

Fearing, Percy. "Non-graded Foreign Languages Classes," *Foreign Language Annals*, March 1969, 343–347.

Hair, Donald, et al, "Experiences with Differentiated Staffing," *Today's Education* 58:56–58, March 1969.

Hernick, Michael and Dora Kennedy. "Multi-Level Grouping of Students in the Modern Foreign Language Program," *Foreign Language Annals*, II, No. 2, 200–204.

Hoye, Almon G. "Let's Do Our Thing—Flexibly" (Part of the Proceedings of the Central States Conference on the Teaching of Foreign Languages, Milwaukee, Wisconsin, April 10–12, 1969) *Modern Language Journal*, LIII, No. 7, November 1969, 481–484.

Metcalf, Lawrence E. and Hunt, Maurice P. "Relevance and the

Curriculum." *Phi Delta Kappan*, LI, No. 7, March 1970, 385–389.

Newmark, Gerald. "Making Foreign Language Instruction More Responsive to Individual Differences in Learners." *International Conference: Modern Foreign Language Teaching. Papers and Reports of Groups and Committees. Reprints Part I.* Berlin: Pädagogische Arbeitsstelle and Sekretariat, Pädagogisches Zentrum, 1964, 451–483.

Otto, Frank. "Individualizing Instruction Through Team Teaching," *Hispania*, LI, 473–475.

Politzer, Robert L. "Flexible Scheduling and the Foreign Language Curriculum," *DFL Bulletin*, VII, i, 1967, 6–8.

Rand, M. John and English, Fenwick, "Towards a Differentiated Teaching Staff," *Phi Delta Kappan* XLIX: 264–268, January 1968.

Reinert, Harry. "Practical Guide to Individualization," MLJ, March 1971.

Rogers, Adrienne. "Motivation: The Forgotten Word," *French Review*, XXXIX, 1966, 906–909.

Steiner, Florence. "Performance Objectives in the Teaching of Foreign Languages." *Foreign Language Annals*, III, 4 (May 1970), 579–91.

Sweet, Waldo. "The Continued Development of the Structural Approach," *Didaskalos*, Vol. II, No. 2. 1967.

Terwilliger, Ronald I. "Multi-Grade Proficiency Grouping for Foreign Language Instruction." *The Modern Language Journal*, LIV, 5 (May 1970), 331–33.

Valdman, Albert. "Toward Self-Instruction to Foreign Language Learning," *International Review of Applied Linguistics*, II, 1964, 1–36.

Wilhelms, Fred T. "Priorities in Change Efforts," *Phi Delta Kappan*, LI, No. 7, March 1970, 368–371.

Wood, Fred H. "The McCluer Plan: An Innovative Non-Graded Foreign Language Program," *Modern Language Journal*, LIV, 1970.

POSSIBLE QUESTIONS FOR DISCUSSION AT IN-SERVICE MEETINGS AND WORKSHOPS

A. GOALS AND OBJECTIVES

1. What is the basic goal that you strive to attain for your FL students?
2. For what purpose(s) do most of your students take FLs?

3. What overall teaching and learning objectives would you state for Level I? Level II?
4. What programs would you establish in an effort to meet the needs of students in your school?

B. TEACHING AND LEARNING FOR MASTERY

1. What specific points would you consider as essential for mastery in Level I? Level II? (List required proficiency in the areas of the sound system and grammar structure.)
2. State overall goals for mastery in terms of terminal performance that you want your students to achieve in listening — speaking — reading — writing for Level I–Level II.
3. What is required of the student (what does he need to do) in order to accomplish each of the objectives stated in the previous question?
4. What do you need to do in order to lead the student to the accomplishment of each of the performance objectives?

C. MODULAR SCHEDULING

1. Block out a flexible schedule (20-15″ mods per day), as you would like to see it in your language.
2. What types of FL learning activities would you choose for a large group — small group — independent study and laboratory time?
3. What procedure(s) would you recommend for staffing the flexible schedule that you propose?
4. How would you make it possible for under-achievers or slower students to be recycled during the academic year?
5. What courses might be offered in the FL beyond the FL classroom?

D. INDIVIDUALIZED INSTRUCTION

1. What would you consider to be desirable topics or projects for individual study?
2. What provisions would you make to establish continuing contact with each student involved with individual study?
3. At the beginning of the year, how would you go about diagnosing the needs of students from various feeder schools who have been enrolled in your 2nd-year FL class?
4. What would you request in the way of equipment and material for a learning center that would function as headquarters for laboratory experiences?

E. DIFFERENTIATED STAFFING

1. What mini-courses could the FL staff offer in your school? How could credit be given?
2. What criteria would you suggest for selecting student teachers, interns, and advanced students who would function as assistants on your teaching team?
3. How do you perceive your role as a member of a teaching team utilizing the concept of differentiated staffing?
4. If your school adopted a differentiated staff program, what requests would you make regarding:
    a) the use of space
    b) the use of equipment
    c) the procedures for planning course content and lesson objectives?

LEON A. JAKOBOVITS[2]

V. A Typology of FL Education with Particular Emphasis on Compensatory and Individualized Instruction[1]

Dr. Jakobovits needs very little introduction to members of the foreign-language teaching profession. As author of *Foreign Language Learning: A Psycholinguistic Analysis of the Issues* and numerous articles on psycholinguistics and foreign-language education, he has provided the profession with needed insights about the processes of individualizing foreign-language learning. His widely-acclaimed lectures throughout the United States and Canada have placed him in the forefront of the movement toward effective individualization of foreign-language instruction in American schools.

INTRODUCTION

Dr. Leon Jakobovits, well-known psychologist and foreign-language educator, offers the reader an informative, helpful essay on planning individualized instruction in foreign language. It is obvious that there are many problems to be solved in implementing individualized instruction, and Dr. Jakobovits' advice, if taken seriously, could help to insure the development of sound individualized programs. This editor is grateful to Dr. Jakobovits for allowing us to share his knowledge and contemplation about individualized instruction.

---

[1] Some of the ideas in this paper came to me during my collaboration with Dr. Barbara Gordon on an experimental in-service training workshop for teachers in bilingual education (Dade County, Miami). It is a pleasure to acknowledge her contribution. This paper is based on an address delivered at the Kentucky Foreign Language Conference, Lexington, Ky., April 1971.

[2] Beginning September 1971, with the Department of Psychology, University of Hawaii, Honolulu, Hawaii 96822.

Discussions on FL teaching methodology usually consist of partisan statements and arguments in which the purported advantages of one method are juxtaposed to the alleged disadvantages of another, with a view to convincing the reader or listener to adopt one and abandon or stay away from the other. This procedure is considered acceptable and ordinary, and I for one, have often engaged in this kind of polemics (e.g., Jakobovits, 1970a, b).

At the time of this writing, in the Spring of 1971, I feel that the polemical climate in FL education is beginning to change somewhat and I would like to attempt a different approach to this perennial problem that concerns us so much. Although there remain amidst us staunch method adversaries enlisted in one cause or another, my impression is that a great number of FL teachers hold a pragmatic view that is both eclectic and sound; they are not committed to a particular theoretical point of view and are willing to experiment with "whatever seems to work." I consider this an encouraging development which is more likely to benefit the students than is the rigid adherence to a particular paradigm. Consequently, I would like, in this paper, to present a comparative analysis of FL teaching procedures that might help delineate their major characteristics. My attitude in this presentation can be characterized by the statement that no one approach is in and of itself superior to any other, but that some might be more suitable than others depending on the circumstances. My analysis will try to specify the relationship between the features of the teaching procedures and these teaching circumstances. What I am aiming for, then, is a *context-dependent* analysis of FL teaching procedures.

THE EBTA CUBE

I would like to begin by proposing three basic distinctions that characterize the various FL teaching procedures: nonprogrammed versus programmed instruction, mass versus individualized instruction, and traditional versus compensatory instruction. Let us take up each of these in turn and examine their characteristics, the major assumptions and premises that underlie them, and some of their implications.

NON-PROGRAMMED VS. PROGRAMMED INSTRUCTION

To me the most salient differentiating feature between programmed and non-programmed instruction is the extent to which the content of a "lesson" is broken up into small unitary "steps" each to be acquired separately and sequentially. Programmed instruction often has associated with it special "hardware" paraphernalia (e.g., "teaching machines"), but I consider these coincidental (not, however, unimportant or irrelevant), and there exist programmed courses which use textbook-type materials for the presentation of the program. "Self-pacing" is often a built-in feature of programmed courses, but in most cases individual differences in rate of learning are not directly taken into account by the internal structure of the program, and translate instead, into how long it takes an individual to complete a "lesson" and consequently, the overall course. Individual differences in learning style are usually not taken into account. Some programs, for instance, will provide short-cuts for the fast learner and elaborations of some steps for the slow learner, while using the same principle of presentation in both instances. Programmed instruction insures acquisition by the very act of completion of the program by the student, and special achievement and performance tests for the course are thus not required. Every student who *completes* his programmed course or "module" is automatically considered to have been "successful". Finally, although programmed instruction constitutes "individual" instruction par excellence, in the sense that the student is alone with his mechanical or textual "teacher", it does not necessarily represent "individualized" instruction as characterized below.

The traditional justification for programmed instruction is the assumption that it is easier to learn small, clear, isolated steps, one at a time, than more or less large, inductively obscure principles. The major problem in programmed instruction has been the difficulty of breaking up the overall content of a skill or course into such specific steps ("frames"). Programmed courses thus vary in validity (the relationship between the steps in the program taken as a whole and the ultimate competence to be achieved), in efficiency (the relationship between how fast and with how many errors an individual acquires competence and his theoretical aptitude or ability), and in interest (the attitudinal and motivational "cost" to the student).

The implications of the development of programmed instruction for education are quite serious and significant, although not necessarily in all aspects of education. Competencies associated with some particular "school subjects" may be more amenable to handling with programmed instruction than others, and they may be more significant with certain types of students than others (e.g., the slow and fast learners versus the "average" student). In my opinion, programmed instruction today faces the same kind of challenge that non-programmed instruction has faced for a long time, which is to combine it with compensatory and individualized principles of instruction (see below).

Mass versus Individualized Instruction

The fact of mass education, its existence and presence in our, and other, technological societies is not a result of merely the emergent need of educating large numbers of people. In its present form, it is no less a result of certain specific assumptions about the learning process and the intended educational objectives. I think this observation is notable because too often educators attempt to rationalize many recognized shortcomings of the educational system by saying that they are the result of an overflow of student population in our schools (or, alternately, an underflow of "qualified" teachers). Certainly it is understandable that overflows and underflows reduce the efficiency of a system. But an increasing number of people have come to believe that some of these shortcomings are to be attributed to the assumptions and principles of the learning-teaching process, and have advocated different, often contradictory assumptions and principles. I would like to refer to this difference by the mass-versus-individualized contrast.

Mass instruction assumes that effective teaching is possible when a group of individuals are brought together in a classroom or laboratory and treated as multiple copies of one ("average") individual ("lockstep"). A relatively pure instance of this approach is basic army training; a contaminated instance is the typical large American graduate school—and there are shades in-between. This basic assumption has several corollaries, the most important ones being the following: graduates of the training program have similar minimal competencies and they can be made to learn in similar sequential and cumulative steps.

The major assumption of mass instruction is contradicted by the individualized approach which treats each individual as a different species of learner. This difference is analogous to the contrast between mass-produced and custom-built automobiles. Note that the principles and opportunities of mass production constitute a technological and economic reality which is what makes it possible to have custom-built automobiles. Similarly, the reality of a public educational system, with its software of teachings and curricula, and its hardware of classrooms and laboratories, makes it possible to have individualized instruction (which should not be confused with one-to-one teaching).

As with orders for custom-built cars, each individual learner is considered a unique and separate problem: graduates of training programs do *not* have similar minimal competencies and they can *not* be made to learn in similar sequential and cumulative steps. These beliefs lead to very different decisions about curricular content and development and to very different expectations about achievement, performance, and competence. Here, the notion of self-pacing assumes less trivial, more critical importance than in many current programmed instruction courses. Here, examinations and tests are not geared to the school year, and "grade level" is not synonymous with age. The conceptions of "teacher", "classroom", and "homework" become less neat and well defined; instead, we may speak of "tutor" or "facilitator" and more simply "work" rather than "class work" or "homework".

TRADITIONAL VERSUS COMPENSATORY INSTRUCTION

We come here to a distinction I wish to make that is likely to create more difficulties than the other two, partly because the word "traditional" ordinarily includes such a broad range of things, and partly because I have previously used the phrase "compensatory instruction" (Jakobovits, 1970a, Chapter 3) where, according to the more refined terminology presented in this paper, I would use "Compensatory-individualized instruction". I believe that the additional differentiation is useful and worth the effort.

Traditional instruction makes the following traditional assumptions: that formal education prepares the individual for the "real life" problems outside school; that courses and curricula provide specialized knowledge and skills which, in their aggregate, constitute professional or work-setting competence; that the discrete skills and knowledge which make up the content of courses and textbooks are to be selected on the basis of some sort of sampling distribution (in terms of their "importance", "frequency", "usefulness", "prerequisiteness", etc.), since they are too numerous to be taught in their entirety; that acquisition of a minimum specified number of such facts and skills constitutes ipso facto evidence of the acquisition of the specialized competence; that the specialized competence which is the purported goal of the instruction process can be adequately defined in terms of these discrete skills, which is to say, independently of the performer and the context of his performance.

Compensatory instruction specifically denies the validity of these assumptions of discreteness, of sampling, of sequential accumulation, of the quid pro quo of formal instruction and competence. The school is not considered as either a substitute or a preparation ground for society "out there," but is taken for its face value as a place *in* society, like the home, or the work setting, which individuals of a certain age are forced to attend, in which they must work and cope to survive as a part of their social and human condition. The school is thus a training and preparation ground only in the trivial sense that the home, the church, the neighborhood, the Boy Scouts, or whatever are training grounds. This is a trivial sense since every decade of an individual's life can be looked upon as preparation for the decades that come afterward.

If you look upon the school in this latter way, then the courses and curricula you encounter there would no doubt still provide specialized knowledge and skills but whether, in their aggregate, they constitute professional or civic competence is an open question to be carefully assessed rather than granted by definition. Similarly, it becomes a problem for demonstration whether professional or civic competence can develop in any other way but by doing and living professionally and civicly. Furthermore, since our specific understanding of real life situations has always been immeasurably less than our understanding of abstract, theoretic, and artificial systems it remains to be shown that an effective formal instruction process, which requires specificity of knowledge, is at all possible under such conditions. Thus, that people can learn, is an undeniable fact of life; that people can teach, is an interesting hypothesis, but an uncertain one.

I have now completed my elaboration of the three binary distinctions of basic approaches to teaching. Since each dimension has been independently defined, we have a possible total of eight basic approaches to teaching. These can be arranged in a

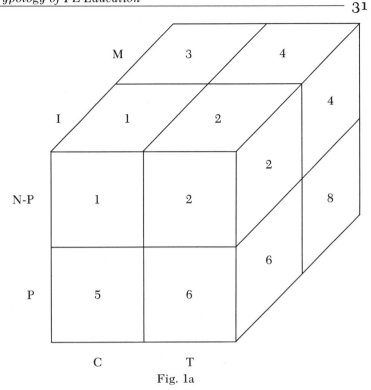

Fig. 1a

Non-programmed				Programmed			
Individualized		Mass		Individualized		Mass	
Comp.	Trad.	Comp.	Trad.	Comp.	Trad.	Comp.	Trad.
1	2	3	4	5	6	7	8

Fig. 1b
Eight Basic Approaches to Teaching: The *EBTA* Cube

three-dimensional cubic figure, as in Fig. 1a, or a two-dimensional figure, as in Fig. 1b. I would now like to discuss the characteristics of a FL curriculum within such a model.

FL INSTRUCTION WITHIN THE EBTA CUBE

In this second half of my paper I am going to adopt a more argumentative style because I believe that fundamental changes are needed in the approaches to FL teaching which characterize many FL curricula in our public educational system at all three levels. Programmed instruction is not yet widespread in education, generally, and in FL instruction, it is used very infrequently, as far as I am aware. Individualized instruction in FL teaching is even more recent a development, although there are signs that an increasing number of individual teachers have taken upon themselves the task of implementing some of its principles in their classrooms (see Altman, 1971, Rogers, 1969). Compensatory instruction is not yet a reality anywhere in the public educational system, but I shall try to argue that we have the know-how to start implementing many of its principles. That leaves the non-programmed–mass–traditional approach (type 4 in Fig. 1) as the standard prototype practically everywhere. This approach, as defined in the first half of this paper, makes the following assumptions (in this, I am going to restrict my focus to the learning and teaching of a second language):

1. The teaching objectives of the language course are stated in very general terms such as "a speaking knowledge" or "a knowledge of 'the four' basic skills", rather than in specific terms as defined by a learning program. Furthermore, there is no need to break up the knowledge that is to be acquired into the strictly unitary steps of a programmed sequence.

2. With some exceptions (such as remedial classes), learners are treated alike in the overall instructional process.

3. Graduates of a FL course or program have similar minimal competence in the second language as attested by the obtention of at least a passing grade.

4. Individuals can learn a second language by going through similar sequential and cumulative steps as defined by the content of a set of lessons variously organized depending on the particular text or method being used.

5. The FL course prepares the individual for the use of the target language outside the classroom or laboratory.

6. Communicative competence can be broken up into discrete skills and "pieces" of knowledge for more efficient learning, and these discrete elements constitute the content of lessons, laboratory exercises, and homework.

7. The degree of communicative competence acquired is directly related to and assessed by the quality of performance on achievement tests (standardized or examination type) which sample attained knowledge of discrete elements presented in the lessons.

8. Communicative competence or knowledge of the language is defined in abstract, generalized, context-free terms.

Assumption (1) derives from the earlier discussion on non-programmed versus programmed instruction. Assumptions (2) to (4) relate to the distinction I have made between mass and individualized instruction, and (5) to (8) derive from the traditional-compensatory contrast. On the basis of my evaluation of the language-learning process or the development of communicative competence (see Jakobovits, 1970a, c), I have come to believe that, with the possible exception of the first (see discussion below), the assumptions associated with the mass-traditional approach are unsound. The following arguments substantiating my impression can also be looked upon as a characterization of the individualized-compensatory approach to language teaching (non-programmed or programmed).

I start with the general premise, often stated by Carroll (e.g., 1965, p. 22) that students in a FL class learn, if anything, precisely what they are taught. This assertion can be interpreted at two different levels, both of which I believe to be valid. At one level, an audiolingual course that emphasizes "oral skills" will show higher achievement scores on tests of listening and speaking performance than a "traditional" course that emphasizes reading and writing, and at the same time, it will show lower scores on tests of reading and writing as compared to the "traditional" course. At another level, one that is not discussed to the same extent in the FL teaching literature, the language skills acquired in the classroom or laboratory will be different from the language skills needed for communicative competence outside the school. That these represent different skills is attested by the common observation that the relationship between success on language achievement tests or course grades and the success in communicating in the target language in real life situations is weak. This weak relationship also holds in the reverse situation where individuals who have learned a second language "in the streets" and have success in communicating in it, do not necessarily obtain high scores on standardized achievement tests.

A corollary to this basic assumption is that the development of communicative competence occurs only in learning situations where there is a real communicative need, and in response to it. The classroom and the laboratory in the context of formal education constitute a social setting where the communicative needs are different from those in nonschool settings. This means that the school achiever will develop a pattern of communicative competence that is different from and not suitable for meeting the communicative needs outside the school. I am not arguing here that the school context is irrelevant; only that it is irrelevant to a significant number of non-school contexts. For instance a formal course in History may be relevant to contributing to our understanding of the historical process as viewed within an academic frame of reference, but its relevance to understanding the daily events reported on the front page of a newspaper, is unconvincing. The study of Latin may be relevant to an understanding of Latin and Ancient Roman civilization, but its relevance to anything else is a moot point. Similarly, the study of a FL in the classroom may develop certain worthwhile knowledge, but its relevance to the use of that language for communicative purposes outside the school appears to be small (e.g., see Carroll, 1968).

Let me argue now in more specific terms. It is generally accepted in FL education today that the development of listening comprehension skills is a highly specific affair and that students must be exposed to fluent native-like speech to be able to understand a native speaker of the target language (as, for instance, a foreign movie or radio broadcast). But this principle is overlooked in most of the other communicative functions of language. For instance, it is generally assumed that asking and answering questions in a pattern practice exercise or a simulated dialogue on the content of a lesson serves to develop the skills needed in asking and answering questions in a real conversation or communicative setting. This expectation is contradicted not only by the daily experience of the FL teacher, but as well, on account of a theoretical analysis of simulated classroom dialogues and real ones. The ability to ask and answer questions is dependent not only on the knowledge of the relevant vocabulary and syntactic patterns but also on background knowledge about the social rules or conventions of conversational interaction and on inferences about intent, appropriateness, and the like. For instance, one does not ask a stranger's name when he has just identified himself to another speaker in our presence. Consider the following conversational sequence:

A1. How long have you been in Montreal?
B1. Three months. And you?
A2. Ah, I'm an old resident of Montreal. We moved here when I was a child. And how do you like it so far?

B2. Well, it's different. I never lived in a large cosmopolitan city before. I imagine it takes people a while to get used to the hustle and bustle . . .

A3. Well, yes. Where have you lived before?

B3. In Quebec City. It's much quieter there and the population is more homogeneous. Mostly French Canadian, you know.

A4. I don't know Quebec very well. . . . Do *you* have any children?

B4. Two boys and a girl. They all go to Gardenview Elementary.

Note that the question in A1 is appropriate only if A has reasons to believe that B is a newcomer to the city. The question in B1 has no such implications, yet it is appropriate in response to A's question. The question in A2 is permissible as a retort to the earlier answer in B1. Had A1 and B1 not preceded it, this question would have been phrased differently and in such a way as to refer to the missing part by means of some sort of elliptical reference to the missing part (e.g., "Well, I understand you are a recent arrival to our city. How do you like it so far?"). Note that A3 contains an assent to a question that is only implied, not stated, in A2 (e.g., "I imagine . . . bustle . . . Don't you think so?"). And so on for the rest of the sequence.

Now consider an analogous conversational sequence in a simulated classroom dialogue.

A1. How long have you been in Montreal?

B1. Three months.

A2. How do you like it so far?

B2. I like it very much.

A3. Where have you lived before?

B3. In Quebec City.

A4. Do you have any children?

B4. Yes.

A5. How many?

B5. Three.

A6. Boys or girls?

B6. Two boys and one girl.

This second sequence is not merely more stilted, more unnatural, more forced; a different organizational sequence underlies the conversation, one that is appropriate in another communicative context (e.g., interview situations where B "submits" to A's questioning for whatever particular reason).

I have given a fairly trivial example, but I hope it illustrates my point. I shall not go into any further details here, but think of the wide range of conversational encounters where differences of this sort become evident: asking for information, expressing an opinion, reporting an event, elaborating a statement, justifying an assertion, explaining, making small-talk, joking, complimenting, subtly disagreeing, appearing unprejudiced, and so on, to the full range of everyday, ordinary, commonplace conversational interaction.

FL educators, when presented with arguments such as these, often reply that "liberated expression" is only to be expected at more advanced stages of language learning, that in elementary language training one must first go through the admittedly artificial exercises of pattern practice and classroom dialogues. I question the soundness of this sequential hypothesis that considers the elementary exercises either a prerequisite to "liberated expression" or, a simpler, more basic, more elementary form of it. I am confident that a communication analysis of the typical classroom interaction will show it up as being no less complex than ordinary conversational interaction, but different from it. Certainly it is the case that the "street produced" bilingual learns the rules of ordinary conversation without going through the so-called elementary, non-ordinary classroom conversational pattern.

Let me summarize my argument thus far. The classroom represents a non-ordinary, specialized communicative setting, with its own complex rules of conversational interaction and specialized functions for language use (e.g., instruction and problem solving). Ordinary commonplace conversational interaction has its own and a different complex set of rules, and it cannot be replicated or simulated in the classroom. The communicative competence that underlies it can only be developed in real life situations.

The FL educators and teachers who become convinced of the validity of this argument will be faced with the necessity of making certain difficult, exploratory, but, I think exciting, decisions that will radically change the contemporary spectrum of the FL curriculum. It will be a change away from the mass-traditional approach to the compensatory-individualized approach. The extent of displacement they may achieve as a result of these new policy decisions will no doubt vary with the existing social, political, and administrative conditions of each school community. This is as it is — but the crucially important point is that each decision that is made, no matter how small in consequences, be of such character as to move the spectrum of FL instruction away from type 4 in the EBTA cube (mass-traditional) to types 1 and 5 (compensatory-individualized). I would like to suggest some major policy decisions that have this character.

1. *The diversification of the FL curriculum while simultaneously restricting the instructional objectives of particular courses within the curriculum* (see also my discussion in Jakobovits, 1970b and 1970a, Chapter 5). Traditionally stated objectives such as "a knowledge of the language" or "a knowledge of 'the four' basic skills" are euphemisms for goallessness and confusion. Instead, objectives ought to be stated within three major functional types, (a) ordinary commonplace conversational use; (b) monadic language use; and (c) non-ordinary specialized language use. Specialized courses with restricted focus may be offered within each of the three major types. Thus, within the type of ordinary commonplace conversational use, there will be courses or sections with "how to . . ." titles in the following form: How to Speak to Strangers in French; How to Shop in Japanese; How to Make Friends in Russian; How to Travel in Spanish; and so on. Within the monadic language use type, courses having rather solitary objectives can be specified in the following form: How to Read Classical Literature in Arabic; How to Write Business Letters in Hebrew; How to Enjoy Indian Movies; How to Listen to French Canadian News Broadcasts; How to Decode Chinese Propaganda Leaflets; How to Pray in Tibetan; and so on. Finally, within the type of non-ordinary specialized language use we would have the following: How to Study Chemistry in German; How to be an English-Albanian Simultaneous Translator; How to Talk to Your French Teacher; How to be a Comedian in Italian; How to Give the Impression of Being a Multilingual Person; and so on.

I hope these rather comical titles do not discourage the serious FL teacher who is contemplating a move toward compensatory-individualized instruction. I allow myself a little bit of humor in an area too devoid of it. Why does FL learning and teaching have to be such a grimly serious and painful enterprise? Think of how much fun students would have in a course entitled "How to be a Comedian in Italian". And think how much of the Italian language and culture they would learn in such a course, even if they failed the Italian Cooperative Listening Comprehension

Test. Naturally, the FL teacher would be hard pressed to find a textbook on Italian Humor for Second-Language Learners, Level 1. But who needs it? I would much rather trust the intuitions of the Italian FL teacher who appreciates Pasta, Mama, and Don Giovani.

2. *Grades in FL courses ought to be based more on the individual student's involvement than on his performance on achievement tests.* By student involvement I mean to refer to the extent to which he engages in the following activities: helping to determine the nature and objective of the course, both contentwise and proceduralwise; helping to determine assessment procedures and evaluation criteria for progress and substantive achievement; assuming responsibility for their own learning and course related activities; making decisions about the languages taught and the overall shape of the FL curriculum; and so on. This type of student involvement gets us away from the perennial and unproductive problem of "How to motivate the FL student" for the simple reason that unmotivated students under the conditions I am describing would not be caught alive in a FL course. Carl Rogers, the famous clinical psychologist-educator has described in moving terms the beautiful relationship that a teacher can have with his students under conditions which I would describe as compensatory-individualized. In his recent book *Freedom to Learn* (Rogers, 1969), he describes various 'contracts' which the teacher-facilitator and the students can draw up at the beginning of the course to insure this type of student involvement. It is a text that I recommend to all educators, parents, and students in any educational field of endeavor.

3. *Student counselling ought to form an integral part of the FL curriculum.* In a previous paper (Jakobovits, 1971a), I have elaborated six premises which form the psychological bases of second-language learning. These were as follows: (1) bilingualism entails biculturalism; (2) bilingualism cannot as a rule be achieved in the FL classroom; (3) there are valid educational objectives in learning a second language that are other than the attainment of bilingualism; (4) learning a second language has associated with it factors and considerations that are unique to it and are different from learning other school subjects; (5) when a large proportion of students fail to learn a second language in school, their "failure" is not a reflection of the teacher's competence or the method he uses; and (6) the condi-

tions that hold under a mass educational system are unfavorable to the development of an effective FL curriculum. Learning is a sacred and sublime activity. It ought to be respected for what it is, namely a very personal and intimate affair. Language learning is particularly important and special because it is the contact point between the individual and his social and physical environment. Individuals vary in interest, ability, aptitude, attitude, motivation, and problem-solving style. The school ought not to be a place where the individual merely learns, but also a place where the individual discovers why he learns and how he learns. This cannot be accomplished in our present classrooms where students are treated as mechanical pawns in a giant educational factory. I would advocate the establishment of small encounter groups (see, for instance, my description in Jakobovits, 1970d) with the FL curriculum which would provide them with the opportunity of examining their attitudes and learning styles in the study of a second language. These encounter sessions can serve to establish a personal and human relationship between the FL teacher and student, can serve as the occasion for drawing up the course contract, and can create a greater awareness of the self as a learner and the psychological implications and consequences of bilingualism and biculturalism. The educational commitment, as I see it, must always be centered in the development of the individual rather than in the acquisition of a predetermined body of knowledge or set of skills.

EDUCATIONAL SLOGANS AND THE SEQUENTIAL HYPOTHESIS

The field of education ordinarily operates within and by means of educational slogans (see Gordon, 1971). These slogans are represented by folk-theoretic explanations given by teachers and other educators for existing practices and diagnostic activities. Here are some examples: "Students are not working up to their abilities"; "FL instruction is designed to teach the students to communicate in a second language"; "The problem is how to motivate the students"; "I use method x to teach"; "Basic patterns and vocabulary must precede free expression", and so on. The justification of educational slogans (their rationality versus their superstitious application) is a topic not unlike that of the emperor's clothes in the children's story: there is a silent conspiracy (negative contract) not to mention it. I am particularly interested here in the sequential hypothesis. This hypothesis has become so ingrained in the very conception of language teaching that it is seldom remembered that this is a *hypothesis* rather than a self-evident truth, so much so that questioning its implications strikes many teachers as odd. But consider.

A child learning a first language is ordinarily exposed to the full range of syntactic patterns of the language of adults and although there is such a thing as "baby talk" that some adults use in interacting with young infants, there is no evidence that this adjustment pattern or anything else that anxious middle-class parents do to "speed up" language development has any significant effect on the child (see Smith and Miller, 1966; Lenneberg, 1967). This experience shows that language *can* be learned contrary to the sequence hypothesized in the basic patterns and vocabulary hypothesis. If you think that second-language learning is different from first-language acquisition in this respect, then think of the common fact that many individuals who are immersed in a culture (e.g., immigrants) come to develop communicative competence in the second language in the absence of a formal instruction procedure that is guided by the sequential hypothesis.

In the light of these two common observations, you might wish to change the sequential hypothesis such that it is a hypothesis about the most effective procedure of learning a second language *in school.* But what evidence do you have that this is indeed so? What is an alternative hypothesis? You might say, for instance, that students will learn, if anything, precisely what they are being taught. If they are taught basic patterns and vocabulary in artificially structured verbal interactions, they will be able to perform under those conditions, but they will not be able to interact in ordinary communicative interactions. The expectation of transfer from the first to second communicative setting has too often remained unfulfilled to deserve continued faith. Why not *begin* the teaching of a language at the second level, in those cases where communicative competence in free conversational interaction is the goal, rather than hope it will materialize by itself in later stages or reserve the practice of it for "more advanced" language learning stages?

Note that the very notion of "basic" patterns and vocabulary is a weakly defined one. Anyone who has transcribed tape-recorded versions of free speech must be convinced that we do not ordinarily speak in alternating "sentences" of the type one practices in classroom exercises and simulated dialogues. It is possible, of course, to write an elementary text in such a way that it contains x number of patterns and y number of words and to practice artificial dialogues containing no more than the particular patterns and words in the "basic" text. But this is possible only because what is being said and how it is said is artificially restricted *in advance.* Even the simplest of free communicative interchanges, however, do not subscribe to this artificial restriction, and it is not a source of much satisfaction to realize that say, 80% of what is ordinarily done in free speech will be subsumed under the "basic" patterns and vocabulary since it takes the other 20% to successfully transact any conversation.

Rejection of the sequential hypothesis does not necessarily imply the absence of any structure in teaching, even though it is true that, at the moment, we do not know precisely how to systematize the instruction of free conversational competence. This is not because the latter type of structured instruction is inherently more complex and difficult to achieve, but because we have not focused in our past research and teaching on the systematic organized nature of ordinary conversations, and until we do so we shall remain hesitant and ineffective in our teaching of it (for a start in this, see Sacks, 1971 and the discussion in Jakobovits, 1971b).

Anyone who cares to think about it would realize that language is used for many different purposes and in many varieties and registers. These different functions and varieties have different, partially independent, underlying skills and competencies and it is naive to think that the same basic hypothesis about teaching procedures can effectively meet the various learning needs in their development. The traditional classification of the "four basic skills" into listening, speaking, reading, and writing categories seems totally inadequate in the light of recent discoveries in sociolinguistics and ethnomethodology (Ervin-Tripp, 1967; Garfinkel, 1968; Sacks, 1971; Searle, 1969). A more realistic approach would take into account the functions and varieties of language as defined by the context in which the language is to be used: ordinary conversational interaction, using language for instructional purposes, reading for pleasure, writing business correspondence, and so on. A realistic goal for our current educational objectives in FL instruction would be for the curriculum to establish three separate and independent "tracks": one track for ordinary conversational interaction, another for reading, and a third for instructional use. Each track would be made up of a flexible package of mini-courses or modules, each worth a certain amount of credit points upon completion. Students should be counseled which track to take on the basis of diagnostically evaluated assessment procedures including aptitude, time and opportunity available for study, interest, learning style and perceived goals (see my discussion in Jakobovits, 1970a, Chapter 3). The procedures and materials to be used with each track ought to be developed by the FL teacher in accordance with a specification of the skills to be acquired. It is important to choose fairly specific terminal behaviors, defined by communicative context and setting, and begin training under those conditions *at the outset* rather than under some allegedly prior or basic but artificial conditions.

The FL teacher is the person who must implement these changes. The prevailing hesitancy of the FL teacher in implementing changes and his dependence on methods and commercially available courses must be actively discouraged by FL administrators and supervisors. For over twenty years now, the FL profession has encouraged this kind of dependence, and if it had been effective it should have been more successful than it has in fact been (see Carroll, 1968). It's time for a swing of the pendulum in a totally different direction, in the assertion of the teacher's role as the one who makes the instructional decisions. Nothing short of this is compatible with the professional responsibility and personal integrity of the teacher.

PROGRAMMED FL INSTRUCTION

The role which programmed instruction can play in FL teaching needs careful evaluation. I stated earlier that the programmed-mass-traditional approach (type 8 in the EBTA cube) can involve the same difficulties and shortcomings that we find in the non-programmed-mass-traditional approach (type 4). The challenge of developing programmed FL courses lies in the application of programming principles to those of individualized and compensatory instruction. If that can be done, I would gladly relabel the sides of the EBTA cube in such a way as to make type 5 into 'number one'. At first blush it would seem that nothing could be more antithetical to individualized and compensatory instruction than the image of a student sitting in a solitary cubicle pressing the buttons of a teaching machine or computer console. I would hate to elaborate such an Orwellian scene. However, it is the case that even within the context of our present impersonal educational institutions some students seem to be functioning well with programmed courses. Hail to them! It seems to me that within the context of individualized and compensatory instruction, the principles of programmed teaching can serve a useful and unique function. Where there is a need for brute force rote memorization, programmed materials can be very handy and efficient. A learning program consisting of small conversational sub-routines can be both interesting and helpful. Furthermore, teaching programs can serve to diagnose learning problems through error analysis, and can provide additional individual practice when needed. Finally, in the absence of other educational opportunities (such as a FL teacher in a particular language), the programmed laboratory can play an essential function in strengthening the FL curriculum.

I am restating with the above comments some of the ordinary things we say today about teaching machines and programmed instruction. It might be worth exploring some non-ordinary things we can say about a programmed FL curriculum. I might start with the following statement: a program is a theory about the structure of knowledge and the process of its apprehension by the human mind. A language-learning program would thus be made up of three sorts of things. One will be a descriptive grammar of the language laid out in a matrix that can form the blueprint for a sequence of linear and branching frames and modules. The second will be a set of specific hypotheses about a learner's inferential and problem solving activities. And the third will be a set of general principles concerning the storage and retrieval mechanisms of the mind. The total number of frames is likely to be a very large number although the number of frames used by any individual learner would be a much smaller number, the actual size varying greatly from one learner to another. The construction of frames would be guided by aspects of the three sets of things just mentioned: the descriptive grammar in matrix form will guide the areas to be covered, one or more frames for each rule or point of grammar; the content and form of each frame will additionally be influenced by the programmer's hypotheses about how various learners apprehend grammatical inferences, inductively and deductively. At this stage, a number of alternative frames arranged in branching sequence will be constructed for each point of grammar, these alternative forms being guided by expected variations in style of inferential behavior. These alternative branches will serve as remedial or compensatory devices during the execution of the program by individual learners. Finally, the frames will be arranged in a structured grid of interconnecting access points in such a way as to provide sufficient practice for storage and retrieval in the mind of the learner while simultaneously excluding unnecessary steps. If you look at the program steps from the first frame to the last as an inferential maze, then the actual route taken by each individual learner will be potentially different from that of any other learner, being determined exclusively by learner characteristics in congruence with the principles of compensatory and individualized instruction.

Now let me return to the Orwellian image once again. Would such a program be equivalent to having a language teacher or could it possibly replace the language teacher altogether? This question reminds me of the robot stories in science fiction literature. In one of these, as I recall, human-like robots were constructed and their outward physical similarity to humans was so perfect that they were actually indistinguishable from real humans. Furthermore, their artificial 'positron' brains were functional duplicates of human brains. Is a robot that is indistinguishable from a human a robot, or is it another human? Is a program that can duplicate the environment a teacher can provide a program or is it a teacher? Posing the problem in these terms makes it obvious that we are not asking a for-real question. Perhaps we should ask, more profitably, what is it about the environment a teacher can provide that is different from the environment the program can provide, and is this difference relevant for the competence that the learner is to acquire? Here we must distinguish between two sorts of programs: if we are thinking of a 'fantastic' program, by which I mean one that can talk and think like a human, then it is obvious that the program will be at least equivalent to the teacher, and probably much better. But at this stage of our knowledge, this kind of program remains truly a fantasy, even to the point where it is not at all clear whether it could ever become a reality. If we are thinking of 'real' programs, by which I mean not only those that our present technology might generate, but as well, future foreseeable technologies, then what such a program would be lacking would be that which any ordinary speaker could provide, namely the opportunity of carrying out an ordinary conversation. Thus, it is now conceivable that a programmed FL course in combination with exposure to ordinary speakers of the language could be at least equivalent to and possibly better than the FL teacher. Now this conclusion is obviously not satisfactory since experience shows that a FL can now be learned solely as a result of exposure to ordinary speakers of the language in the absence of either a programmed FL course or a FL teacher. So the question of the machine versus the teacher remains unresolved. And maybe this is as it should be.

No doubt a more practical question is, what the program can do for the FL teacher and the FL learner? I think the usual answer which says that the program can free the teacher from routine tasks involved in rote memorization and practice drills, while probably true and not inconsequential, is nevertheless selling the program short. It overlooks the fact that programmed modules of limited scope can facilitate the learning process in ways that are completely beyond the capacity of the human teacher. Individualized, compensatory and remedial instruction must be responsive to individual differences in style and rate of learn-ing in such a way as to provide the opportunity for exposure to a sufficient number of alternative branching sequences of frames that is far beyond the attention span and control of a human teacher, yet it provides no special problem for even our presently available hardware in computer-assisted instruction. It is true that we do not have many comprehensive programs available at the present time, but I think this is less because of an absence of know-how than the absence of practice and development. For one, the hardware associated with computer-assisted instruction is very expensive and beyond the range of most educational establishments. For another, most teachers have not shown any interest in contributing to the development of such instructional programs, not even the simple kind that need no special hard-ware or expensive hardware. It is here that I feel that a change in attitude on the part of FL teachers would be most useful and productive (see Howatt, 1969, for useful hints).

There are two large areas of the EBTA cube with which I have not dealt so far, namely the individualized-traditional (type 2 or 6) and the mass-compensatory (type 3 or 7) approaches. As individualized instruction gains in prominence and popularity, we will see interesting attempts to apply it within the context of traditional objectives: the teaching of a pre-determined package of discrete elements of knowledge tailor-made to the individual learner, particularly in the form of programmed instruction (type 6). I suspect that the majority of FL teachers today could see themselves working under such conditions. The mass-compensatory combination is more problematic. It is the typology that some so-called "free schools" follow today: the exposure in school to a set of pre-determined uniform conditions with the expectation of similar minimal attainment and similar sequential cumulative acquisition steps, but not defining these conditions in terms of the usual course content. It retains the age-graded promotion idea while at the same time rejecting textbooks and traditional subject area divisions.

I have now completed my journey through the EBTA cube and I hope it has served a facilitating, rather than a befuddling function, a new way perhaps of discussing the problems and challenges that face FL education today.

INITIATING CHANGE: THE EBTAMOBILE TRIP

In this final section, I would like to make more specific suggestions as to the kind of changes in FL instruction that I think are desirable. The EBTA cube represents a way of talking about the philosophy of teaching that is basic and general. How does movement take place within the EBTA cube, say if we wish to move from the top right-hand corner (type 4) to the bottom left-hand corner? A method of translocomotion occurs to me which I shall briefly describe, but given its presently unrefined character, I hope it will be taken not as a method to be applied, but rather a method to be discussed. I shall call this proposed solution to the problem of initiating change in basic approaches to teaching as the Triadic Method of Least Resistance and the ensuing profile of the instructional changes as the Ebtamobile Path.

Step 1. List the instructional areas in which you believe you have some degree of control. I would like to suggest the following seven general headlines:

    A. The shape of the overall curriculum
    B. Course content and materials
    C. Classroom activities and assignments
    D. Type of tests and their timing
    E. Nature of grading system
    F. Distribution of time and work modules
    G. Opportunity for diagnostic and remedial activities

Step 2. Get together with administrators and supervisors and discuss all alternatives that occur to you in these instructional areas in connection with the following four directions of change:

    1. Ratio of student/non-student initiated acts
    2. Specificity of student contract
    3. Degree of self-pacing
    4. Nature of student/teacher interaction

TABLE 1. THE TRIADIC METHOD OF LEAST RESISTANCE
Steps 1–4: The theoretically possible paths: 280 changes

	1	2	3	4
A. The shape of the overall curriculum 1 2 3 4 5 6 7 8 9 10				
B. Course content and materials				
C. Classroom activities and assignments				
D. Type of tests and their timing				
E. Nature of grading system				
F. Distribution of time and work modules				
G. Opportunity for diagnostic and remedial activity				

1 = Ratio of student/non-student initiated acts
2 = Specificity of student contract
3 = Degree of self-pacing
4 = Nature of student/teacher interaction (degree of facilitation; empathic understanding)

Steps 5–6: Draw line above geometric average of stress points in each box between teacher/administrator/student, and implement.

Theoretically, you have a 7x4 matrix of 28 boxes which are independent of one another (see Table 1). For instance, for area A (The shape of the overall curriculum), the ratio of student initiated acts may be quite low, whereas it may be quite high in areas D or F. The degree of self-pacing may be substantial in area F and insignificant in area D. A specific contract may be *drawn up* between the student and the teacher in area D but *imposed* by the teacher in area B. By "Nature of student/teacher interaction" I have in mind particularly two scales: (i) teacher as authority figure vs. teacher as tutor or facilitator and, (ii) high vs. low empathic understanding between student and teacher (see Barrett-Lennard, 1962).

Step 3. Get together with the students and discuss these alternatives with them, noting whatever additional suggestions they may have.

Step 4. Make a list of possible changes within each of the 28 boxes and arrange them in a rank order of extent of departure from current practices such that the change in rank position 1 would be minimal and that in position 10 (say) would be fundamental, with 5 being "somewhat rocking the boat but not pulling down the roof over your head." You end up with a matrix list of 280 changes (10 changes within each of the 28 boxes). This grid of 280 change items constitutes the possible theoretical path of the ebtamobile. To determine the actual path that is possible for you, with your particular students and in your particular school at any particular time, figure out the path of least resistance as follows.

Step 5. Draw a line *above* the first change item in each of the 28 boxes which represents for you the point of psychological stress, that is a change that you cannot live with comfortably if you were to function under those conditions. In some boxes, your stress point may be at rank 2; in others, you may be courageous enough to go down to rank 6 or 7. You end up with 28 scores for yourself, varying between 1 and 10 (if you used a ten-point scale). This is your psychological change profile. Now determine in a similar way the psychological change profile for your supervisor, and also for each of your students if you are committed to an advanced individualized instruction program, or, if you are working in a mass-oriented environment, use the average student psychological change profile for the class. Determine the path of least resistance by computing a geometric average for the three psychological change profiles. This will give you the context-specific instructional profile that is possible in your school at this time.

Step 6. Implement immediately all the change items in each of the 28 boxes that fall above the line of the path of least resistance.

And Presto!—you are well on your way towards an individualized program. A cautionary note: it should be good practice to recompute the path of least resistance at the beginning of each semester.

REFERENCES

Altman, H. B. Toward a definition of individualized foreign language instruction. *American Foreign Language Teacher*, February 1971, No. 3.

Barrett-Lennard, G. T. Dimensions of therapist response as causal factors in therapeutic change. *Psychological Monographs*, 1962, 76. (Whole Issue No. 562.)

Carroll, J. B. The prediction of success in intensive foreign language training. In Robert Glazer (ed.), *Training Research and Education*. New York: Wiley, 1965.

Carroll, J. B. Foreign language proficiency levels attained by language majors near graduation from college. *Foreign Language Annals*, 1968, 1, 318–353.

Ervin-Tripp, Susan. Sociolinguistics. Working paper no. 3, Language Behavior Research Laboratory, University of California, Berkeley, 1967.

Garfinkel, Harold. Studies in Ethnomethodology. Englewood Cliffs, N.J.: Prentice-Hall, 1968.

Gordon, B. Individualized instruction and sub-cultural differences. Paper presented at the Kentucky Foreign Language Conference, Lexington, Ky., April 1971.

Howatt, A. P. R. *Programmed Learning and the Language Teacher*. London: Longmans, 1969.

Jakobovits, L. A. *Foreign Language Learning: A Psycholinguistic Analysis of the Issues*. Rowley, Mass.: Newbury House Publishers, 1970 a.

Jakobovits, L. A. Motivation and foreign language learning: Part A. Motivation and learner factors. *Report to the 1970 Northeast Conference on the Teaching of Foreign Languages*, 1970 b.

Jakobovits, L. A. Prolegomena to a theory of communicative competence. In Robert C. Lugton (Ed.), *English as a Second Language: Current Issues, Language and the Teacher Series*, Vol. 6. Philadelphia: Center for Curriculum Development, 1970 c.

Jakobovits, L. A. The psychological bases of second language learning. *Language Sciences*, February 1971, 22–28. (a).

Jakobovits, L. A. The Encounter-Communication Workshop. Institute of Communications Research, University of Illinois, Urbana, 1970 d (Mimeo).

Jakobovits, L. A. Towards a psychology of ordinary language. Paper presented at the Central Pennsylvania Psychology Lecture Series, April 1971. (b)

Lenneberg, E. H. *Biological Foundations of Language.* New York: Wiley, 1967.

Rogers, C. R. *Freedom to Learn.* Columbus, Ohio: Charles E. Merrill, 1969.

Sacks, Harvey. *Aspects of the Sequential Organization of Conversation.* (Forthcoming, Prentice-Hall publications, 1971.)

Searle, J. R. *Speech Acts.* Cambridge, England: Cambridge University Press, 1969.

Smith, Frank and Miller, G. A. (Eds.). *The Genesis of Language.* Cambridge: M.I.T. Press, 1966.

VI. The Management of Individualized Programs

John F. Bockman (M.A., Univ. of Arizona, M.A.T., Indiana Univ.) is Coordinator of Foreign Language Instruction, Tucson (Arizona) Public Schools. He has taught Latin, Russian, and German on the high-school level and taught methodology at the Univ. of Illinois EPDA Russian Teachers' Institute, 1969. He has attended NDEA Institutes in the United States and the Soviet Union, and was a participant at the NDEA Foreign Language Leadership Institute at Central Washington State College. He has published many articles in the *Arizona Foreign Language Teachers' Forum* and will serve as Consultant to the Editorial Board for Vol. 3 of the *Britannica Review of Foreign Language Education*. His professional affiliations include the NEA, AATG, and ACTFL.

Valerie M. Bockman is a research specialist and systems analyst and has served as a research associate at the University of Arizona, as well as for several well-known business concerns. She has published articles on management in education and is currently on the staff at Pima College in Arizona.

INTRODUCTION

Mr. John Bockman and Mrs. Valerie Bockman, both experienced in educational management, provide needed guidelines for both the administrator and teacher responsible for individualizing foreign-language learning in the schools. The analysis of the necessary management strategies and practical presentation of alternatives suggest needed changes in thinking directed toward successful individualization of foreign-language instruction.

MANAGEMENT — THE LINK BETWEEN INSTRUCTION AND LEARNING

Management may be thought of as the assortment of "jobs" teachers do which might better be done by others — administrators, secretaries, aides, perhaps even parents. "Teachers should be free to teach" has become a dictum among teachers.

Unless a teacher enjoys chaperoning, policing halls, keeping records, etc., he is likely to regard most managerial assignments as an imposition, if not the bane of his existence.

The teacher's instincts in this matter are, of course, substantially correct. Most management is not his affair. To stay in the business of teaching, however, the teacher must not give up his most important function—the management of learning. To exercise and strengthen this vital function, he may well have to come to view "teaching" as a radically different function from what it has seemed to be in the past.

The dignity, the importance, and certainly the proper understanding of the concept *instructional management* must be restored. The public has come to recognize that proper management is to good learning what appropriate instruction is to good teaching. From long and increasingly sophisticated experience in ever more universal education, the public knows that teaching of subject-matter content without supportive management of learning has resulted either in no learning or in minimal learning for far too many children and adolescents. A school-wise public is fast turning against teaching which seems to take place chiefly for its own sake, in majestic isolation from learning.

The new doctrines of *accountability* dictate that if students fail to learn, their poor attitudes, inadequate backgrounds, cultural differences, economic deprivations, and other contributory causes must no longer be used to absolve the school and the teacher. "They can't be taught" must change to "Their learning will be managed." Beautiful teaching, like exquisite ballet, is a delight to observe, but learning is what the public expects to get for its money.

Even though the management of learning is an essential function of the teacher, the concept is easily misunderstood and frequently misapplied. Evaluation, for example, is a process of the management of learning. Giving grades and entering them in a grade book are comparatively trivial "jobs." Such jobs could be abolished altogether, and good evaluation could well go on. But in the absence of an expected specific evaluation task, how many job-oriented teachers and administrators would believe it? How many equally conditioned parents would accept it?

Frequently the teacher's many "jobs" seem to incapacitate him for performing the real heart of his highest function. Jobs too easily become their own ends, and management as an integral decision-making, instructional function with ends in learning fails to develop. The teacher gets lost in "jobs" because they seem all-important. (Watch a little girl play school!) If the "job" isn't done, there is a visible gap in the teaching. The fact that the job, in the doing, may create a gap in learning is easy to overlook. For too long, educational jobs without significant learning outcomes have escaped censure. That day is past.

Thus it is necessary, first of all, to discriminate carefully between management as an instructional function based in decision making and the many "jobs" a teacher tends to do in trying to discharge it. The notion that management of learning is a miscellaneous collection of jobs or tasks which the teacher does to cause others to learn is rejected. The management of learning will not be that easy to define. It has something to do with wise and logical decisions concerning the best rational arrangement of many disparate things to achieve ends in learning which must somehow be *expected.*

THE FOUNDATION OF GOOD INSTRUCTIONAL MANAGEMENT

In planning to manage individualized or independent study, the teacher would be well advised to hold fast to two fundamental principles:

1. There is little efficient and effective learning in the school setting without efficient and effective instruction;
2. There is little efficient and effective instruction without efficient and effective management.

This says simply that nothing purposeful happens in education, as elsewhere, unless it is caused. These management principles apply to individualized instruction and to independent study just as much as they do to traditional teaching, perhaps more so. Chaos, or the absence of instruction, is not an option. Unfortunately, however, *instruction* is an equivocal term which requires clarification.

Instruction is understood here in its etymological meaning—a building up or erection of an epistemological framework of order, form, and substance which permits and facilitates the functioning of the learning processes. The systematic construction of frameworks for learning within the experiences of the learner encourages learning to occur, just as the erection of an arbor encourages the grapevine to climb. For example, knowledge of terms, facts, and rules; control of applications, translations, analysis, and synthesis; and the growth of appreciation, judgment, and value are all likely to occur, other things being equal, if they are structured in order, form, and substance. Obviously, teaching may be instruction *par excellence* in this sense, but other types of instruction, many of which do not require intervention, mediation, or even presence of a teacher, are not only imaginable, but attainable. Nature, for example, has always been the foremost successful instructor of man's learning experiences. The computer, the programmed textbook, sets of cassettes, or any number of other suitably organized systems may play the same role as nature or the teacher.

The image of instruction as the erection of a framework which encourages learning suggests a counter-image—the erection of an anti-framework which encourages no learning. Both of these acts can take place in the name of teaching. Thus teaching may be instruction, but not necessarily. Some teaching may not be instruction at all. The concept of instruction is broader than the concept of teaching. In individualized instruction, the applications of teaching in its usual meaning must obviously change, but to say this is neither to demean teaching nor to deny its rightful place in the educational processes.

Two Dilemmas of Instructional Management

Since the art of teaching first developed its contradictions, good teachers have wrestled with two dilemmas concerning a balance in their functions. The dilemmas have never been so acute and universal as they are today. Social and technological changes have suddenly created a Protean age—one in which almost anything can become almost anything else at almost any time (Arendt 2). As Hanzeli and Love (12) express it, foreign-language teachers today are galaxies away from their concerns of just yesterday. Change was rapid in the generations immediately preceding ours, but the present painful fact is that the *nature* of change has changed (Strasheim 16). Educators must find ways not just to live with change, but to cope quickly with changed change.

The first dilemma facing today's teacher is:

> Paternalism and autocracy in the teaching act are now inappropriate and increasingly unacceptable; but an abdication of critical functions and accountability by competent teachers will not be tolerated by society.

To resolve the dilemma, instructional management must
1. Reduce or eliminate the inordinate domination of learning by the teacher; and, at the same time,
2. Preserve all the critical functions and the accountability of the teacher.

The second dilemma facing today's teacher is:

Universal learning must be made accessible to all; yet excellence of performance must be achieved, both in some absolute sense and to the highest level of individual capability.

To resolve the second dilemma, instructional management must
1. Proportion educational opportunity almost exactly to the capability of the learner; and, at the same time,
2. Promote excellence of achievement absolutely and in terms of individual capability (Bockman, J. F. 6).

Because of the critical state education finds itself in today, for reasons which have been well explored through the media and in national best sellers, it is especially important that facilitation of learning, wherever possible, replace teaching, and that individualization and personalization of teaching, wherever possible, replace mass teaching (Jacobovits 13). Facilitation, individualization, and personalization of instruction through good management procedures seem to offer American education its only hope of resolving its present serious dilemmas.

IMPORTANCE OF TEACHER ATTITUDES IN FACILITATION, INDIVIDUALIZATION, AND PERSONALIZATION OF INSTRUCTIONAL PROCESSES

In individualized instruction, as previously suggested, the concept of good classroom management must yield to the concept of good learning management through instruction both in and out of the classroom environment. Good learning management depends, if possible, even more on teacher attitudes than on management procedures (Altman 1). Especially important, therefore, are the aspects of teacher attitudes which have a close bearing on good management procedures.

Two divergent models of sets of attitudes proposed by human-behavior theorist Douglas McGregor (14) are helpful in differentiating traditional management (and traditional teaching) from humanistic management, the type of management which seems called for in individualized instruction:

The traditional manager's (and traditional educator's) view of people in general (Theory X) is that they:

1. Dislike and avoid work (study);
2. Must be coerced, controlled, directed, and threatened with punishment to get them to direct their efforts toward achievement of organization (educational) goals; and
3. Prefer to be directed, wish to avoid responsibility, have little ambition, and want security above all (Bockman, V. M. 10).

Teachers wishing to individualize instruction frequently find the above behaviors characteristic of large numbers of students. The same sort of resistance to objectives of management occurs in industry and is widely deplored. McGregor maintained that this behavior pattern, rather than being a consequence of man's inherent nature, results from management's philosophy, policy, and practice (Elbing II). Traditional management, then, confuses cause and effect, and would appear actually to condition a "Theory X" response from those being managed in this manner. Traditional educational practice, as well, often seems to have conditioned students to behave according to this model.

McGregor also formulated what he called "Theory Y," which he believed to be a more realistic assessment of people in general, even though it often seems to violate the experience of classroom teachers and others in management roles. According to "Theory Y," students, and people in general,

1. Regard mental and physical work as natural as play or rest;
2. Exercise self-control and self-direction;
3. Are committed to objectives because of the rewards of achievement;
4. Accept and seek responsibility; and
5. Exercise a high degree of imagination, ingenuity, and creativity in solving problems (Bockman, V. M. 10).

It is frequently distressing to teachers wishing to individualize instruction that students do not always behave according to the humanistic model. It will be immediately noted, of course, that "good" students have always exhibited "Theory Y" characteristics, while the majority of students have not. If "Theory Y" is a correct assessment of human nature, however, and not just the description of a set of rare phenomena, it would appear that something in the structuring of learning experiences and something in the attitudes of teachers may be contributing to the problems of managing *all* students by the humanistic model.

A very practical first consideration in adopting the humanistic approach would be, of course, that individual behavior exists along a maturity continuum, the extremes of which are described by Chris Argyris:

Infancy --*Maturity*
1. Passivity ---Activity
2. Dependence ---Independence
3. Behaving in a few ways-------Behaving in many different ways
4. Erratic, casual, shallow,
    quickly-dropped interests-----------------------Deeper interests
5. Short time perspective--------------------Longer time perspective
6. Subordinate position-----------------------Superordinate position
7. Lack of awareness of self----Awareness of and control over self

(Any given student at a given time will place at some different point along each of the above continua.)

By its very nature, traditional management demands submissiveness, passivity, dependency, short time perspective, and repetitive shallow abilities. The more mature the individual being traditionally managed, the more likely he is to become frustrated and to adapt to the situation by becoming apathetic or indifferent (Argyris 3). The teacher's management of individualized learning also will be subject to the constraints imposed by the variety of students' positions along the above continua.

Frederick Herzberg's ideas about the duality of man's nature may help to define the precise differences between attitudes contributing to "Theory X" behavior and attitudes contributing to "Theory Y" behavior (Bockman, V. M. 9). This, in turn, may help justify the "mix" of traditional and humanistic procedures that may be required by a realistic assessment of the constraints imposed by students' positions on the maturity continua in any given environment.

The habitual seeking of pain-avoidance mechanisms (or hygiene factors, as Herzberg calls them), such as
    tangible reward (grades),
    good interpersonal relations (socialization in the school
        environment),
    supervision (good teacher-student relationships),
    liberal school regulations,
    comfortable and attractive surroundings and study conditions, etc., to the exclusion of other things is characteristic of "Theory X" behavior conditioned by traditional management

attitudes toward people. It is not suggested that pain-avoidance mechanisms are undesirable. This point can best be illustrated by psychologist Abraham Maslow's (15) hierarchy of needs:

1. Basic physiological needs
2. Safety
3. Love
4. Esteem
5. Self-actualization

Each set of needs must be satisfied to some extent before the next becomes activated, and as it is reasonably well satisfied, it loses its potency as a prime motivator of behavior. Since the needs for pain-avoidance mechanisms are classified at the lower portions of Maslow's hierarchy, it is evident that without their fulfillment, higher needs could not become activated. But it is also evident that a mere superabundance of such hygiene factors cannot *satisfy* higher needs. Thus, the mere "pile-up" of socialization, liberal regulations, good interpersonal relations, good working conditions, and general over-all permissiveness does *not* solve root management problems.

On the other hand, factors leading to "Theory Y" behavior are characterized by Herzberg as "motivators" or growth mechanisms:

The work itself,
achievement,
recognition,
responsibility, and
advancement

are factors leading to growth—the satisfaction of a higher order of needs. The management required in individualized instruction is of the "motivator" variety. This is so because individualization cannot succeed if the student will not assume a large part, perhaps all, of the responsibility for his own instruction. Apparently, however, growth cannot be imposed—it must be self-activated under conditions which allow it to happen. Thus, efforts to impose growth also do *not* solve root management problems.

McGregor points out that to be properly motivated toward organizational (here, educational) goal achievement, the member must accept the organization's goals as his own, or they must coincide with his personal goals to some extent. One of the best ways to achieve such a coincidence of goals is through the member's participation in goal formation. Quite in keeping with humanistic management attitudes, such participation would help to foster growth and to encourage maturity of behavior. Quite evidently, therefore, participation in goal formation creates conditions which allow growth factors to become operable.

In comparing these two sets of attitudes and their related mechanisms ("Theory X" and traditional vs. "Theory Y" and humanistic), it seems clear that eliminating grades, supervision, regulations, and administration, and strengthening socialization and freedom from constraints of various kinds are *not* going to change "Theory X" students into "Theory Y" students. The elimination of traditional management practices may simply remove the structure, i.e., the instruction, which has allowed learning of even a minimal sort to take place. In some innovative educational programs, traditional structure seems to have given way to *no* structure, almost *anti*-structure, in the guise of freedom to pursue individual educational objectives, and a general permissive state described currently as "doing your own thing." Traditional instruction must be judged far superior to this sort of subverted individualized "instruction," the chief mark of which is, indeed, the inexcusable absence of instruction.

The management theories of McGregor and Herzberg, among others, would suggest that if individualization is to be efficient, effective, and accountable, one kind of structure, super-imposed, must be replaced by another kind of structure, self-imposed, not by a state of no structure.

It would seem that teacher attitudes contributing to effective facilitation and personalization of learning in individualized instruction are almost necessarily humanistic. Traditional attitudes would seem to militate strongly against the very concepts of facilitation and individualization because traditional attitudes imply that students cannot be trusted to direct their own efforts toward educational goals. On the other hand, humanistic attitudes do not require elimination of instruction, structure, form, and substance, as many may suppose. Humanistic management, if it really intends to lead to maximum learning, must be just as concerned with these things. The difference lies in recognizing the vital role of the student in achieving them.

Realistically, some aspects of traditional instructional procedures, without the traditional attitudes, might well have to be retained in some measure in a highly effective individualized study program because of the maturity continua mentioned above. Especially when one is modifying structure for highly dependency-conditioned students, it is wise to remember that as in remodeling a building, the less structural disturbance, the better. The treatment of students may constitute the larger difference.

Good management, then, based on "Theory Y" attitudes, would seem to require:

1. A careful analysis of the many variables that exist in a given environment, including students' positions on the maturity continua; and
2. The wise making of decisions to choose one or the other structural component to conform to each major variable.

In the process, the good manager erects an integrated system of both "Theory X" and "Theory Y" procedures which adapts itself flexibly to the unique needs of each individual student. It should always be understood, of course, that those needs may be met only within the constraints of the given environment.

AN ANALYSIS OF MANAGEMENT PROCESSES

The logical flow of almost any imaginable individualized program from conception to implementation suggests the following sets of processes (Bockman, J. F. 8):

1. The teacher responsibly creates a new learning environment.
2. The student responsibly enters the new learning environment.
3. The teacher and other agents, including the students, responsibly sustain the new learning environment.
4. Educators and others share responsibility for guiding students through the new learning environment toward excellent learning outcomes.
5. Educators and students arrange for the responsible use of physical, material, and human resources to sustain the new learning environment.
6. Educators responsibly evaluate student and program strengths and weaknesses and provide for recycling or modification as needed.
7. Educators responsibly modify all aspects of the new learning environment as needed.
8. Educators ensure that the pertinent rights of the individual student, his peers, his parents, society at large, and the educational institution are adequately safeguarded (Bockman, J. F. 7).

An adaptation of the above analysis was submitted to an in-service planning committee of public school teachers who used the first seven steps as the basis of an in-service seminar series in individualized instruction management (Tucson Public Schools 17).

A questionnaire (Bockman, J. F. 8) was designed to elicit answers which it was believed any thoughtful and reasonable student, parent, educator, administrator, or taxpayer would have a right to expect of any teacher initiating and implementing an individualized or independent study program. It was placed at the disposal of the planning committee which, in turn, submitted pertinent parts of it to the chairmen of the seven sessions of the seminar for their consideration.

A modified form of the questionnaire is partially analyzed below with suggested management decisions as they might be made in several different hypothetical school environments. For each of the first three sets of processes, the order of the analysis is as follows:

A. Alternative judgments
B. Discussion of the hypothetical school environment
   1. Factors favorable to individualization
   2. Factors unfavorable to individualization
C. Management decisions
D. Analysis of management decisions

Only sample Alternative Judgments are provided for the last four sets of management processes. The reader is invited to make his own management decisions in view of the unique nature of his own school environment.

I. THE CREATION OF AN INDIVIDUALIZED LEARNING ENVIRONMENT

A. *Alternative Judgments*

1. The program will be $\left\{\begin{matrix} \text{required of} \\ \text{elected by} \end{matrix}\right\}$ students.

2. The program will be offered $\left\{\begin{matrix} \text{with} \\ \text{without} \end{matrix}\right\}$ special steps to motivate students.

3. The program will be offered $\left\{\begin{matrix} \text{only to academically talented} \\ \text{to both talented and untalented} \end{matrix}\right\}$ students

4. The program $\begin{Bmatrix} \text{will} \\ \text{will not} \end{Bmatrix}$ be allowed to proved irresponsible students.

5. The teacher will $\begin{cases} \text{specify the objectives.} \\ \text{allow the students to determine the objectives.} \end{cases}$

6. The teacher $\begin{Bmatrix} \text{will} \\ \text{will not} \end{Bmatrix}$ aid the students in developing objectives.

7. The teacher will $\begin{Bmatrix} \text{allow} \\ \text{deny} \end{Bmatrix}$ students the right to modify objectives.

8. The teacher will $\begin{Bmatrix} \text{allow} \\ \text{deny} \end{Bmatrix}$ students the right to reject teacher-made objectives.

9. The teacher will regard the program as $\begin{cases} \text{a totally new learn-} \\ \text{ing environment.} \\ \text{a mere realignment} \\ \text{of roles.} \end{cases}$

10. The teacher $\begin{Bmatrix} \text{will} \\ \text{will not} \end{Bmatrix}$ develop a system of records.

11. Students $\begin{Bmatrix} \text{will} \\ \text{will not} \end{Bmatrix}$ have access to certain records.

12. The rigidity of the schedule $\begin{Bmatrix} \text{will} \\ \text{will not} \end{Bmatrix}$ be modified.

13. Certain specific abuses will be tolerated under $\begin{cases} \text{given conditions.} \\ \text{no conditions.} \end{cases}$

14. Genuine independence will be $\begin{cases} \text{granted.} \\ \text{restricted.} \end{cases}$

15. Students will be trusted $\begin{cases} \text{completely.} \\ \text{under certain given conditions} \\ \text{of supervision.} \end{cases}$

16. Students $\begin{Bmatrix} \text{will} \\ \text{will not} \end{Bmatrix}$ be systematically aided in developing good independent study habits.

B. Discussion of Hypothetical School Environment #1

1. Factors favorable to individualization
   a. Innovative principal
   b. Innovative and helpful curriculum coordinator from central staff

   c. Loose articulation of programs within the school
   d. Freedom to innovate
   e. "Theory Y" attitudes of the teacher
   f. Experience of the teacher
   g. Support of a large group of parents
   h. Support of a University program
   i. Assistance of District research, measurement and evaluation, and pupil services department with their specialized personnel

2. Factors unfavorable to individualization
   a. No time flexibility
   b. Limited space flexibility
   c. No assistance from aides or other teachers
   d. Fairly rigid code of discipline
   e. Strongly dependent, relatively immature student body
   f. Rigid grading system
   g. "Traditional" colleagues
   h. Rigid "traditional" community expectations

C. Management Decisions.

An analysis of factors, favorable and unfavorable, suggests the following characteristics of a new learning environment in this school:

The program will be elected by students *(1)* . . . because they are self-motivated *(2)* . . . are academically talented and responsible *(3 and 4)* . . . and can and will determine their own objectives *(5)* . . . . The teacher will aid the students in determining their objectives *(6)* . . . which may be modified at any time at the option of the students, if the modification is duly recorded *(7)* . . . . Students are free to reject all teacher-made objectives *(8)* . . . . Students engage in self-instruction with the teacher in the role of consultant—perhaps a realignment of roles rather than a totally new learning environment *(9)* . . . . The teacher will develop a system of records *(10)* . . . to which the students will have complete and immediate access *(11)* . . . . The schedule will not be modified, but time may be spent outside the assigned classroom *(12)* . . . . No abuses will be tolerated for any reason, even to permit an adjustment to independent learning *(13)* . . . but students are given genuine independence *(14)* . . . and are trusted so long as they do not abuse their contractual agreements with the teacher *(15)* . . . . Students are given some help in developing good independent study habits, but for the most part these are assumed to exist, because the teacher does not have time to work carefully with each individual to achieve this end. Therefore, offending students are summarily dismissed from the program (*16*).

Analysis of Management Decisions

The above decisions show a good mix of "Theory X" and "Theory Y", with humanistic attitudes generally dominant. The mix recognizes the existing constraints, the need to safeguard against abuses in the existing school and community environments and the need to secure structure for the promotion of good learning. Since the structure is chiefly formed by the students, "Theory Y" conditions will probably prevail. "Theory X" controls appear to be applied primarily to ensure that immature students will in fact develop the structure necessary for learning. They do not appear to be applied for repression or suppression of structure developed independently by students.

II. Student Entry into the New Learning Environment

A. Alternative Judgments

1. The individual student $\begin{Bmatrix} \text{can} \\ \text{cannot} \end{Bmatrix}$ profit from the individualized study opportunity.

2. The student $\begin{Bmatrix} \text{does} \\ \text{does not} \end{Bmatrix}$ have the personal resources to make this a worthwhile learning experience.

3. The student $\begin{Bmatrix} \text{can} \\ \text{cannot} \end{Bmatrix}$ set his own learning objectives.

4. The student $\begin{Bmatrix} \text{will} \\ \text{will not} \end{Bmatrix}$ need a given amount of time to adjust to independent learning.

5. If the student flounders or fails to adjust to independent learning within a given amount of time, some specific person $\begin{Bmatrix} \text{will} \\ \text{will not} \end{Bmatrix}$ be ready to help him.

6. The student $\begin{Bmatrix} \text{will} \\ \text{will not} \end{Bmatrix}$ be left for a period of time without assistance.

7. The student $\begin{Bmatrix} \text{does} \\ \text{does not} \end{Bmatrix}$ understand the role of an independent learner.

8. The student $\begin{Bmatrix} \text{has} \\ \text{has not} \end{Bmatrix}$ accepted the role of an independent learner.

9. The interacting roles of all the participants in the individualized program $\begin{Bmatrix} \text{have} \\ \text{have not} \end{Bmatrix}$ been differentiated.

10. The roles of all others who may become involved $\begin{Bmatrix} \text{have} \\ \text{have not} \end{Bmatrix}$ been considered. The consent of all potential participants, including volunteers, $\begin{Bmatrix} \text{has} \\ \text{has not} \end{Bmatrix}$ been procured.

11. $\begin{Bmatrix} \text{One person is responsible} \\ \text{More than one person shares responsibility} \end{Bmatrix}$ for supervising the program.

12. If the responsibility is shared, it $\begin{Bmatrix} \text{has} \\ \text{has not} \end{Bmatrix}$ been analyzed and recorded.

13. Unanimity in serious matters $\begin{Bmatrix} \text{does} \\ \text{does not} \end{Bmatrix}$ exist among all who share responsibility.

14. Circumstances require that $\begin{Bmatrix} \text{one person assume a high degree of risk.} \\ \text{several persons assume an equal risk.} \end{Bmatrix}$

15. Written information concerning rights and responsibilities $\begin{Bmatrix} \text{is} \\ \text{is not} \end{Bmatrix}$ put into the hands of students.

16. Parents $\begin{Bmatrix} \text{have} \\ \text{have not} \end{Bmatrix}$ been advised of the details of the program.

17. Parents $\begin{Bmatrix} \text{have} \\ \text{have not} \end{Bmatrix}$ consented to the details of the program.

18. There $\begin{Bmatrix} \text{has} \\ \text{has not} \end{Bmatrix}$ been a contractual process.

19. There $\begin{Bmatrix} \text{is} \\ \text{is not} \end{Bmatrix}$ a contract instrument.

20. The student $\begin{Bmatrix} \text{has} \\ \text{has not} \end{Bmatrix}$ been thoroughly indoctrinated in the nature of the program, his responsibilities, and the risks, if any.

21. The student $\begin{Bmatrix} \text{has} \\ \text{has not} \end{Bmatrix}$ been required to make a commitment to the program.

22. All potential risks $\begin{Bmatrix} \text{have} \\ \text{have not} \end{Bmatrix}$ been thought out.

23. The student and his parents $\begin{Bmatrix} \text{do} \\ \text{do not} \end{Bmatrix}$ know how his work will be evaluated and by whom.

24. There $\begin{Bmatrix} \text{is} \\ \text{is not} \end{Bmatrix}$ a record of parental reaction to the evaluation plans.

25. Parents $\begin{Bmatrix} \text{have} \\ \text{have not} \end{Bmatrix}$ had an opportunity to express reservations about the program.

26. Parents $\begin{Bmatrix} \text{have} \\ \text{have not} \end{Bmatrix}$ been satisfied that rights will not be violated.

27. Reservations of parents $\begin{Bmatrix} \text{will} \\ \text{will not} \end{Bmatrix}$ be given consideration.

B. Discussion of Hypothetical School Environment #2

1. Factors favorable to individualization
   a. Teacher with "Theory Y" attitudes
   b. Support from an innovative college professor
   c. Wide spread of ability within the student body
   d. Paucity of class sets of instructional materials
   e. Good selection of library materials
   f. Librarian with "Theory Y" attitudes
2. Factors unfavorable to individualization
   a. "Traditional" principal
   b. Centrally determined traditional curriculum
   c. State-adopted textbooks
   d. Rigid authoritarian school and community environments with stress on control
   e. Emphasis on standardized test results
   f. Little or no centralized resources
   g. Teacher's relative inexperience with individualized instruction

C. Management Decisions

Individual students who are intelligent, motivated, and self-controlled can profit from the individualized study opportunity (*1*) . . . because they *do* have the personal resources (*2*) . . . and *can* set their own learning objectives provided these are regularly approved by the teacher (*3*) . . . . Students will require little time to adjust to individualized instruction, since the environment is carefully controlled (*4*) . . . but if any student flounders, the teacher will aid him immediately or remove him from the individualized study environment if this appears desirable (*5*) . . . . Students will have continuous access to needed assistance (*6*) . . . . The students understand the role of an independent learner within this rather narrow environment. Their understanding of the expected role is tested in a written questionnaire (*7*) . . . . Students accept the role by contracting with the teacher in a carefully conducted contractual process (*8 and 18*) . . . . The roles of the teacher, the librarian, and the students in this individualized environment have been carefully detailed in writing for parents and principal (*9*) . . . . Several resource persons in the community may become involved with the students as time goes on. Their roles have been carefully considered and their consent has been secured (*10*) . . . . The teacher and the librarian have agreed to share responsibility for supervision (*11*) . . . but the shared responsibility has not been analyzed and recorded, because it is assumed that no serious problems will develop because of the limited nature of the venture (*12*) . . . . The teacher and the librarian share similar views about important matters in their relationships with "good" students (*13*) . . . . They will assume equal responsibility and accountability (*14*) . . . . Program privileges and constraints are fully described in a manual which is given to each participating student and becomes part of the contract (*15, 18, and 20*) . . . . Parents are informed before students are invited to participate in individualized study (*16*) . . . but parents do not give written consent to their child's participation in the program (*17*) . . . . There is a formal contract instrument, the termination of a contractual process (*19*) . . . . Students must make a strong commitment to the program through the contractual process (*21*) . . . . The teacher has not considered any unusual risks because careful controls would appear to preclude them (*22*) . . . . Parents, principal, teacher, and students all assume that traditional evaluative procedures will be employed. No unusual procedures are planned. Parental reaction to evaluation has not been sought. Parents generally support traditional testing and grading, and these are to be expected in the program (*23* and *24*) . . . . Parents have expressed few reservations about plans for individualized instruction. Some parents are concerned lest their children not be prepared for college in a program which differs somewhat from the traditional (*25*) . . . . Parents have been assured that the education of their children will not be allowed to suffer (*26*) . . . . Any parental concern which might come to light during the program will be acted upon at once.

Analysis of Management Decisions

The above decisions show a mix of "Theory X" and "Theory Y" with traditional attitudes dominant. Quite rigid, "Theory X" control seems necessitated by factors within the environment which the teacher ethically dare not ignore. This sort of individualized program will probably be small and tentative, but may provide the teacher and the school with a base of experience on which a larger individualized program may be safely built in the future. The decisions attempt to ensure a safe, sure structure for learning for students with "Theory Y" attitudes and habits. Good experience may result in broadening the program in the future along lines more consonant with humanistic principles.

III. SUSTAINING THE NEW LEARNING ENVIRONMENT

A. Alternative Judgments

1. The teacher $\begin{Bmatrix} \text{does} \\ \text{does not} \end{Bmatrix}$ develop a strong set-to-learn at the beginning of the program.

2. The teacher $\begin{Bmatrix} \text{does} \\ \text{does not} \end{Bmatrix}$ develop a system for the periodic renewal of motivation.

3. Students $\begin{Bmatrix} \text{are} \\ \text{are not} \end{Bmatrix}$ held responsible for spending scheduled time working in the program.

4. Students $\begin{cases} \text{must spend scheduled time in a set place in} \\ \quad \text{the school building.} \\ \text{may spend predetermined time in a place of} \\ \quad \text{their choice in or out of the school building,} \\ \quad \text{including the community.} \end{cases}$

5. If achievement is demonstrated,
   $\begin{cases} \text{the amount of time spent is regarded as immaterial.} \\ \text{both achievement and time spent must be proved.} \end{cases}$

6. The student $\begin{Bmatrix} \text{is} \\ \text{is not} \end{Bmatrix}$ required to keep a record of time spent in the program.

7. If the program involves skill development, this development $\begin{Bmatrix} \text{is} \\ \text{is not} \end{Bmatrix}$ supervised and evaluated systematically and regularly.

8. There $\begin{Bmatrix} \text{is} \\ \text{is not} \end{Bmatrix}$ a syllabus of learning objectives for both students and teacher to follow.

9. If there is a syllabus of learning objectives, students $\begin{Bmatrix} \text{do} \\ \text{do not} \end{Bmatrix}$ really know what the objectives are.

10. If learning objectives are specified, the students $\begin{Bmatrix} \text{do} \\ \text{do not} \end{Bmatrix}$ have the opportunity to agree to them.

11. Students $\begin{Bmatrix} \text{are} \\ \text{are not} \end{Bmatrix}$ required to keep a record of progress and of objectives achieved.

12. Students $\begin{Bmatrix} \text{do} \\ \text{do not} \end{Bmatrix}$ have a right to modify objectives within the structure proposed by the teacher.

13. If students have a right to modify objectives, a record of the modifications made $\begin{Bmatrix} \text{is} \\ \text{is not} \end{Bmatrix}$ required.

14. Achievement of objectives $\begin{Bmatrix} \text{is} \\ \text{is not} \end{Bmatrix}$ evaluated systematically.

15. How, when, and by whom evaluation is to occur $\begin{Bmatrix} \text{are} \\ \text{are not} \end{Bmatrix}$ specified in detail.

16. Achievement $\begin{Bmatrix} \text{is} \\ \text{is not} \end{Bmatrix}$ recorded by means other than grades, e.g., anecdotal records, attitude scales, etc.

B. Discussion of Hypothetical School Environment #3

1. Factors favorable to individualization
   a. Philosophy of school supporting individualization of instruction

    b. Commitment of principal and majority of teachers to individualization of instruction

    c. Relatively mature student body

    d. Flexible space arrangements within the school

    e. Flexible scheduling arrangements

    f. Support of central supervisory and administrative staff

    g. Receptivity of teachers to in-service education and help of every kind from all sources

    h. Good support from interested University personnel

    i. Support of majority of parents and of the community served by the school

    j. Good publicity from the press

    k. Relatively open campus

2. Factors unfavorable to individualization. (Most factors in this environment favor individualization. The concept has been built into the school's buildings and philosophy. It is accepted, nominally at least, by all members of the administration and faculty.)

    a. Some laissez-faire permissiveness is allowed or encouraged by some members of the faculty.

    b. A majority of the faculty members are determined to write their own instructional materials. Lack of time and experience to do this well have resulted in inferior and inadequate materials in some subject areas.

    c. The school lacks equipment needed for full implementation of the ambitious individualization plans of most members of the faculty.

C. Management Decisions

The teacher concentrates on developing a set-to-learn for the beginning of individualized study (1) . . . and plans renewed motivational activities for strategic points in the school year (2) . . . . Students will be responsible for spending scheduled time working in the program, but this is not interpreted so strictly that most cooperative students will not control their use of most in-school time (3) . . . . Students will spend most of their scheduled time in school, but may easily obtain permission to work outdoors on the school grounds. With adequate controls, they may spend some time away from school in libraries, the University, public buildings, etc. (4) . . . . Students must prove achievement, but time spent is deemphasized except in skill areas where a close check is kept on the amount of time spent in actual study (5) . . . . In skill areas, students must be physically present to spend the scheduled time, or must account for it on a time sheet (6) . . . and all such activity is generally closely supervised and carefully evaluated (7) . . . . A syllabus of learning objectives or Learning Activity Packages are required for each course (8) . . . . Students are to understand what the objectives of each course are (9) . . . . In most courses, students will be expected to accept the objectives of the course by the very act of enrolling (10) . . . . Most courses will use Learning Activity Packages, programmed, or semi-programmed materials which will provide a record of progress and objectives achieved (11) . . . . Students will rarely be given the right to modify course objectives to any significant degree (12) . . . . When students are granted such right, it will generally be granted by informal arrangement with the teacher rather than by written commitment (13) . . . . An effort will be made to evaluate achievement of objectives systematically, but time and experience will not yet permit ideal implementation or formative evaluation (14) . . . . Evaluation will tend to be conducted traditionally, although because of the permissiveness of some teachers, good evaluation will not be a strong factor in some programs (15 and 16).

Analysis of Management Decisions

Almost all decisions in this environment are "Theory Y," although some teachers will make "laissez-faire" decisions in the mistaken belief that these are humanistic, or, at least, decisions required by contemporary conditions. Their permissiveness and lack of good evaluative procedures will appear to cater to the immaturity of a minority of students and may create "Theory X" conditions contrary to the philosophy of the school. Among the results of their decisions may be a distressing amount of aimless wandering around, excessive socialization for its own sake in the open areas and in the library, and the appearance of disorder in some parts of the academic buildings. As the school year progresses, "permissive" teachers will be encouraged by colleagues and administrators to recognize that their promotion of un-structure may be leading to "Theory X" behavior, not "Theory Y" behavior, as they may have supposed. On the whole, however, there will be evidence that "Theory Y" decisions of the majority of the faculty are leading through student responsibility and independence of study to good learning outcomes.

In the analysis of the sets of processes which follow, the reader is invited to make management decisions which are based on factors within the environment of his own school.

IV. SHARED EDUCATOR RESPONSIBILITY FOR GUIDING STUDENTS TOWARD LEARNING OUTCOMES

Alternative Judgments

1. Supervision of an individualized program is $\left\{\begin{array}{l}\text{an individual}\\\text{a shared}\end{array}\right\}$ matter.

2. Other affected persons, e.g., librarians, $\left\{\begin{array}{l}\text{are}\\\text{are not}\end{array}\right\}$ involved in planning and decision-making.

3. Affected persons $\left\{\begin{array}{l}\text{are}\\\text{are not}\end{array}\right\}$ philosophically opposed to the concept of individualized study as it is implemented in this program.

4. Some more or less unwilling person $\left\{\begin{array}{l}\text{is}\\\text{is not}\end{array}\right\}$ expected to assume a major share of supervisory responsibility.

5. The program $\left\{\begin{array}{l}\text{will}\\\text{will not}\end{array}\right\}$ cause problems for any teacher or administrator not directly connected with it.

6. The program $\left\{\begin{array}{l}\text{is}\\\text{is not}\end{array}\right\}$ being imposed on any teacher, librarian, or administrator.

7. Differentiated roles — counselor, advisor, motivator, teacher, diagnostician, prescriber, record-keeper, resource person, etc. — $\left\{\begin{array}{l}\text{have}\\\text{have not}\end{array}\right\}$ been developed for the supervisory group.

V. ARRANGEMENTS FOR RESPONSIBLE USE OF PHYSICAL, MATERIAL, AND HUMAN RESOURCES TO SUSTAIN THE NEW LEARNING ENVIRONMENT

Alternative Judgments

1. Efforts $\left\{\begin{array}{l}\text{are}\\\text{are not}\end{array}\right\}$ made to create new associations for the new environment — new space, new time arrangements, new ways of relating to students, etc.

2. Materials and equipment $\left\{\begin{array}{l}\text{are}\\\text{are not}\end{array}\right\}$ put within reasonable control of the students.

3. Materials and equipment $\left\{\begin{array}{l}\text{are}\\\text{are not}\end{array}\right\}$ adequate to help attain the objectives of the program.

4. Extra-school resources $\begin{Bmatrix} \text{are} \\ \text{are not} \end{Bmatrix}$ conveniently available.

5. Library resources $\begin{Bmatrix} \text{have} \\ \text{have not} \end{Bmatrix}$ been taken for granted in planning the program.

6. The librarian $\begin{Bmatrix} \text{does} \\ \text{does not} \end{Bmatrix}$ retain certain discretionary rights which could significantly modify the program for a given student.

7. The rights of all potential resource persons within the school $\begin{Bmatrix} \text{have} \\ \text{have not} \end{Bmatrix}$ been anticipated and protected.

8. Access to resource persons $\begin{Bmatrix} \text{will} \\ \text{will not} \end{Bmatrix}$ be controlled.

9. All potential resource persons $\begin{Bmatrix} \text{do} \\ \text{do not} \end{Bmatrix}$ have an adequate understanding of the program and their proposed role in it.

10. A major supervisory role $\begin{Bmatrix} \text{does} \\ \text{does not} \end{Bmatrix}$ fall on any resource person.

11 .The library $\begin{Bmatrix} \text{is} \\ \text{is not} \end{Bmatrix}$ the only place outside the classroom where individualized study can be conducted.

12. Space in the school $\begin{Bmatrix} \text{does} \\ \text{does not} \end{Bmatrix}$ offer convenient, quiet study opportunity.

13. Space and time inadequacies $\begin{Bmatrix} \text{have} \\ \text{have not} \end{Bmatrix}$ been identified and compensated for.

VI. RESPONSIBLE EVALUATION OF STUDENT AND PROGRAM STRENGTHS AND WEAKNESSES
   Alternative Judgments

1. Pre- and post-testing procedures $\begin{Bmatrix} \text{will} \\ \text{will not} \end{Bmatrix}$ be employed.

2. The program $\begin{Bmatrix} \text{will} \\ \text{will not} \end{Bmatrix}$ provide a means for student self-evaluation.

3. The relationship between evaluation and announced objectives $\begin{Bmatrix} \text{will} \\ \text{will not} \end{Bmatrix}$ be analyzed and used in reforming the program.

4. There $\begin{Bmatrix} \text{will} \\ \text{will not} \end{Bmatrix}$ be a carefully explained grading policy.

5. Students $\begin{Bmatrix} \text{will} \\ \text{will not} \end{Bmatrix}$ be involved in determining their own grades.

6. Evaluation, other than grades, $\begin{Bmatrix} \text{will} \\ \text{will not} \end{Bmatrix}$ be reported to parents, administrators, and counselors.

7. Anecdotal records $\begin{Bmatrix} \text{will} \\ \text{will not} \end{Bmatrix}$ be kept.

8. Evaluation $\begin{Bmatrix} \text{will} \\ \text{will not} \end{Bmatrix}$ be systematically discussed with students.

9. Feedback from students $\begin{Bmatrix} \text{will} \\ \text{will not} \end{Bmatrix}$ be systematically collected, processed, and used in reforming the program.

10. The program $\begin{Bmatrix} \text{will} \\ \text{will not} \end{Bmatrix}$ be evaluated by an extra-school research agency, e.g., the District research department.

VII. RESPONSIBLE MODIFICATION OF THE NEW LEARNING ENVIRONMENT

Alternative Judgments

1. The student $\begin{Bmatrix} \text{will} \\ \text{will not} \end{Bmatrix}$ be permitted to exit at once from a proved unsuitable individualized learning environment.

2. Radical changes in the environment $\begin{Bmatrix} \text{may} \\ \text{may not} \end{Bmatrix}$ be made once the program is launched.

3. Student attitudes $\begin{Bmatrix} \text{will} \\ \text{will not} \end{Bmatrix}$ be measured, and the resulting data $\begin{Bmatrix} \text{will} \\ \text{will not} \end{Bmatrix}$ be used to modify the environment.

4. Student attitudes $\begin{Bmatrix} \text{will} \\ \text{will not} \end{Bmatrix}$ be permitted to modify the objectives in the ongoing program.

5. The program $\begin{Bmatrix} \text{does} \\ \text{does not} \end{Bmatrix}$ recognize the students' need for rest and reassessment.

6. The environment $\begin{Bmatrix} \text{does} \\ \text{does not} \end{Bmatrix}$ allow for self-pacing and study by fits and starts rather than by orderly progression.

7. Critical problems $\begin{Bmatrix} \text{have} \\ \text{have not} \end{Bmatrix}$ been anticipated and provided for.

THE TEACHER'S RESPONSE TO MANAGEMENT NEEDS

The planning committee of teachers who considered the above sets of processes involved in the management of individualized instruction presented an in-service seminar proposal to school district personnel, many of whom were alert to the demands of liability and accountability (Bockman, J. F. 5). For an entire semester about seventy teachers and administrators engaged in transactions focusing on management. The in-service seminar culminated in the group writing of guidelines related to each of the seven management processes analyzed above.

It is noteworthy that the following guidelines were developed by a group consisting chiefly of classroom teachers for the use of other classroom teachers:

Guideline 1: New learning environments should be planned with caution, taking due account of the environment of the school. Planning must include all others on the staff who will be affected by it. Communication and feedback should be open and encouraged.

Acceptance of the new learning environment should be sought from *all* groups in the community affected by it.

New learning environments should be created with full recognition of the existing limitations of resources.

Guideline 2: A teacher must be able to draw together sufficient knowledge of learning theory, sufficient knowledge of a wide range of subject matter, sufficient sense of organization, and sufficient experience in dealing with individuals to ensure reasonable success of the new learning environment.

A student should be called on to make a clear statement of his goals, objectives, and time use constraints to ensure reasonable success of the venture.

Guideline 3: The process of responsibly sustaining a new learning environment depends upon: (a) Use of some record forms, one of which should be a statement of progress in terms of objectives; and (b) The mutual development of records by both teacher and student out of the experience of the project itself. The records should lead the student to further study.

Guideline 4: Given that several educators share a mutual set of students involved in individualized programs, assurances should be made that those educators agree on the students' program objectives and cooperatively coordinate the implementation of activities leading toward competence in those objectives.

Guideline 5: Control of all parameters of the environment to the maximum extent possible is necessary. (N.B. This is a rather extreme statement from the standpoint of "Theory Y" philosophy. It reflects teacher concern that individualization of instruction not degenerate into permissiveness.) This calls for extensive pre-planning for all relationships: teacher-pupil, teacher-librarian, teacher-community resources, pupil-pupil, pupil-librarian, etc.

Guideline 6: Evaluation depends on responsibly established goals and being conscious of them. Assessment goals that are set either too low or too high with respect to the objectives posed fail to help a student responsibly progress through a program. Programs as well as students must be fairly evaluated.

Guideline 7: Provisions for modifying processes should be pre-planned to prevent crises from occurring. It may be desirable, for example, to expect certain kinds of program failures and to develop certain techniques for recycling student learning opportunities, depending on the nature of the program. Definitions should be formulated to distinguish among phenomena which are easily confused. Techniques of observation should be developed to help distinguish among them, e.g., creative thinking, contemplation, needed relaxation, socialization which distracts from learning opportunities, and transactions of various kinds which promote unanticipated learning of a high order.

CONCLUSION

In traditional "Theory X" teaching, the teacher acts upon a mass of from 30 to 40 students called a class, as though it were one mind with 30 to 40 incidental bodies. The managing of learning for a single mind, individual or mass, has not been a terribly complex problem. In fact, however, as has always been perfectly clear, students do not learn *as* a mass. Required to learn *in* a mass, many have always done so quite successfully over the years. Increasingly, however, as enrollment in higher levels of education has become universal, and as excellence or the striving for excellence has become a social imperative, it has become evident that many students cannot or will not learn in mass modes.

Individualized instruction aims to turn a socially intolerable situation around by opening up and encouraging individualized modes of learning. In order to accommodate this sort of change with hope of success, the teacher will have to master a set of fairly complex management techniques. It is reasonable to assume that individualized instruction will require more sophisticated management than traditional teaching. By no means can individualized instruction for large numbers of students succeed without careful management.

In order to master complex management procedures, the teacher may have to change certain fundamental attitudes, specifically from "Theory X," which generally distrusts the individual, to "Theory Y," which generally trusts the individual to be capable of achieving educational objectives which are at once his own and yet perfectly compatible with the expectations of society.

The problems involved in changing attitudes and in mastering new techniques of management are not insoluble. They require, however, careful and continuous analysis of all the factors involved. They require persistent focus on learning as discrete from teaching.

REFERENCES

1. Altman, Howard B. "Individualized Foreign Language Instruction: What Does It Mean?" *Individualization of Foreign Language Learning in America.* II Spring, 1971, p. 14.

2. Arendt, Hannah, quoted in *U.S. News and World Report,* May 19, 1969.

3. Argyris, Chris. *Personality and Organization.* New York: Harper and Row, 1957.

4. Bockman, John F. *Comments in Summary and Evaluation.* Tucson (Arizona) Public Schools, Independent and/or Individualized Study Management Seminar, Final Session, May 17, 1971.

5. Bockman, John F. *Innovative Independent Study Programs and Teacher Liability.* Mimeograph. Tucson (Arizona) Public Schools, 1969.

6. Bockman, John F. *The Process of Contracting in Foreign Language Learning.* A position paper submitted to the conference on Individualizing Foreign Language Instruction. Stanford University, May 6-8, 1971.

7. Bockman, John F. "A System of Instruments for the Management of Independent Study." *Research in Education.* 6:4 (April 1971), p. 62.

8. Bockman, John F. *Tentative Syllabus: Mini-course in the*

    Preparation of Control Instruments and Techniques for Independent Study Programs. Mimeograph. Tucson (Arizona) Public Schools, 1970.

9. Bockman, Valerie M. "The Herzberg Controversy." *Personnel Psychology.* Summer 1971.

10. Bockman, Valerie M. "The Management of Change in Education," University of Arizona. Unpublished paper. Digest to be published under the title, "The Principal as Manager of Change," in a forthcoming issue of *The Bulletin* of the National Association of Secondary School Principals.

11. Elbing, Alvar O. *Behavioral Decisions in Organizations.* Glenview, Illinois: Scott, Foresman and Company, 1970.

12. Hanzeli, Victor E., and Love, William D. *From Individualized Instruction to Individualized Learning.* Preliminary draft. Unpublished, 1971.

13. Jakobovits, Leon A. "Eight Basic Approaches to Teaching: the EBTA Cube." Presentation to Stanford Conference on Individualizing Foreign Language Instruction, May 6-8, 1971.

14. McGregor, Douglas. *The Human Side of Enterprise.* New York: McGraw-Hill Book Company, 1960.

15. Maslow, Abraham. *Motivation and Personality.* New York: Harper & Bros., 1954.

16. Strasheim, Lorraine A. "A Rationale for the Individualization and Personalization of Foreign-Language Instruction." *The Britannica Review of Foreign Language Education,* Vol. 2. Chicago: Encyclopaedia Britannica, Inc., 1970.

17. Tucson Public Schools. Independent and/or Individualized Study Management Seminar, February 8 to May 17, 1971.

VII. A Checklist for Development and Control of Individualized Instruction

INTRODUCTION

Whenever teachers and administrators begin to individualize instruction, they do or should ponder several critical questions. The list of questions provided in this section could prove to be very helpful for anyone who is about to begin an individualized program or who is experiencing difficulties in the process of implementation. Some repetition of items as well as cross-referenced interrogation serve to remind the curriculum planner of the potential pitfalls in individualizing foreign-language instruction.

This writer recommends the checklist, especially since a highly-respected colleague, well-versed in public-school teaching and administration, conceived the format after the latter, himself, had experienced the problems included. If the "neophyte", so to speak, can anticipate many of the problems, he may never have to lose time unnecessarily. Successful individualized foreign-language programs — the goal of many teachers and administrators for the future — may well be achieved months or years faster, if this list is used as it applies to each local school situation.

I. PROCESSES WHEREBY WE ENTER A STUDENT INTO A WORTHWHILE INDIVIDUALIZED STUDY PROGRAM.

1. What evidence makes us think that this student can profit from this opportunity?
2. What and how much and when is this student going to have to contribute to make this a worthwhile experience? Does the student have the resources?
3. What and how much and when is the teacher or originator going to have to contribute to make this a worthwhile experience? Does the teacher or originator have the resources?

4. Is the teacher or originator structuring himself in or out of the program? Why?

5. Who (or what combination of individuals) has structured or will structure the program for the student? What are his (their) credentials?

6. If the student flounders, on whom is the burden of structuring a program going to fall? Is it likely to fall on someone other than the teacher or originator? Will the student be left without assistance? How long?

7. How well does the student understand his role in individualized study? How has this been determined?

8. Has the student really accepted his role? How has this been determined?

9. Have the roles of the student, the teacher, and any others been duly recorded? How? Where are these records? Who has access to them?

10. Have the possible roles of others been considered, e.g., librarians? Has their consent been secured? Have they been taken into account in the anticipation of problems?

11. Is some *one* person responsible for discharging the duties of this program? Who? Are others uninvolved? Why?

12. To what extent and how is the responsibility shared? Is this recorded? Who shares the responsibility?

13. Is there unanimity in serious matters among all who share the responsibility? If not, why not?

14. Do circumstances require that one person more than others assume a high degree of risk? How are others protected if something goes wrong?

15. What written information has been put in the student's hands? Where is this recorded?

16. How have parents been advised? Have they consented? How? Where are the records?

17. Is there a contract? Who wrote it? Where is it?

18. Has the student received a thorough indoctrination in the nature and purpose of the program, his responsibilities, the risks, etc.? How was this done? Is it recorded? Where?

19. Have all potential risks been thought out? Is there a record? Where?

20. Do the student and parents know how the student's work will be evaluated and by whom? Is there a record of parental reaction to this plan?

21. Have parents expressed any reservations about this pro-

gram? Is this recorded? What was done to satisfy parents? Are their reservations to be ignored?

22. Have rules and regulations pertaining to the program; facilities, materials, and equipment to be used; conduct; use of time, etc.; been duly promulgated? How?

II. THE PROCESSES OF RESPONSIBLY CREATING A NEW LEARNING ENVIRONMENT.

1. Has the program been presented to the student as a requirement or as an elective? What is the philosophy behind this?
2. If an elective, has the program been presented on a take-it-or-leave-it basis or has there been a deliberate effort to stimulate and motivate the student?
3. Is there any prestige attached to individualized study in the given environment?
4. Does the opportunity seek the student or does the student seek the opportunity?
5. Must the student be academically talented to enjoy this opportunity? Can an academically talented but irresponsible student study independently, whereas the converse would not be permitted?
6. Is there an effort to develop a strong set-to-learn? How is this done?
7. Has the teacher or originator specified behavioral objectives for the program? What are they?
8. Does the student know that he is expected to achieve these objectives? How is he informed?
9. If objectives have not been specified or communicated, does anyone know what the objectives of the program are? Who?
10. If the student is to develop his own objectives, does he know it? How?
11. Does the student have any skill in developing objectives and in designing a program to reach them? How do we know? Where did he develop this skill?
12. Is there a system for aiding the student in understanding the objectives? What is this system? How does it work?
13. Does the student accept the program's objectives as his own? What is done to secure this?
14. Is it possible for the student to modify the program's objectives? How?
15. Is it possible for the student to reject the program's objectives? If so, what happens next?

16. Is this program thought of as a new learning environment, or as "new wine in an old bottle"? What has been done to create a new learning environment besides modifying traditional roles?
17. Is there a records system? What is it? Where are records kept? Who has access to them? Are there any notable gaps in the records?
18. If the schedule is traditional, what has been done to modify the effects of its rigidity? Are students simply dumped in some central location where they continually distract one another?
19. Are certain "abuses" tolerated? Why?
20. In order to avoid certain abuses, are real independent study opportunities restricted? What is done to secure a balance?
21. To what extent is the student really trusted?
22. To what extent is the student aided in learning independent study habits? How?

III. THE PROCESSES OF RESPONSIBLY SUSTAINING THE NEW LEARNING ENVIRONMENT.

1. For how long is the initial stimulus expected to last? Does the program have a built-in renewal system? What is it and how is it to work?
2. Is the student held accountable for time? Which time? Spent where? Periods of time or cumulative time? School time or home time? How are these determinations to be made?
3. Is the student in violation of a regulation if he spends given time doing something else?
4. Is the expenditure of so much time an essential condition of learning (e.g., it takes anyone at least twenty hours of concentration to develop this skill), or is it relatively immaterial (e.g., one person will grasp a concept instantaneously, whereas another person may never fully grasp the concept)? Has this been analyzed from the standpoint of accountability for time?
5. If time is an essential condition of learning, does the program require keeping a record of time? If not, why not? If so, how is this done?
6. If the program involves skill development, how is this development supervised?
7. Is there a syllabus of learning objectives?

8. Does the student know what these objectives are? Does he have an opportunity to agree to them? How is this accomplished?
9. Does the student have an opportunity to modify certain objectives within the given framework of objectives? How is this done?
10. Is the achievement of objectives evaluated? How? When? By whom?
11. How is achievement recorded and reported?

IV. THE PROCESSES OF CROSS-TEACHER RESPONSIBILITY FOR GUIDING STUDENTS.

1. Is the supervision of this program an individual or a shared matter?
2. What is the make-up of the group sharing supervisory responsibilities?
3. Are there any affected persons whose cooperation has not been specifically solicited, e.g., librarians?
4. Are there any affected persons who have not been involved in planning and in decision-making? Why?
5. Are there any affected persons who are philosophically opposed to individualized study or who have serious misgivings about it? How is this problem to be met?
6. Is any major portion of supervisory responsibility being unwittingly placed upon any more-or-less unwilling person?
7. Will the program unwittingly cause problems for anyone? Is the program unwittingly being imposed on anyone?
8. What has been done to develop a sense of the "shared environment" for individualized study?
9. In the high schools, what has been done to develop departmental rather than individual control of individualized study? Differentiated roles — counselor, advisor, motivator, teacher, diagnostician, record-keeper, resource person, etc.?
10. Does the supervisory group provide a congenial meeting or study place?
11. Is the supervisory group able to keep the various roles distinct depending on need? Is there a tendency to encroach on the student's rights as an independent scholar? How is this assured?
12. Is there substantial agreement in the group concerning evaluation? Is it in writing?

V. RESPONSIBLE USES OF PHYSICAL, MATERIAL, AND HUMAN RESOURCES TO SUSTAIN THE LEARNING ENVIRONMENT.

1. Is an effort made to create new associations for a new learning environment—new space, new time arrangement, new ways of relating to the student? How is this achieved?
2. Are materials and equipment put within the control of the student? How is this done with safeguards?
3. Are materials and equipment reasonably adequate to help attain the objectives of the program? If not, how are deficiencies to be remedied?
4. If the student must go elsewhere for assistance, can this be done conveniently? Have potential resources been consulted in advance?
5. Are the library and its personnel taken for granted or have these resources had an adequate voice in decisions concerning this program?
6. Does the librarian retain certain discretionary rights which could significantly modify the program for a given student? Has this been spelled out for all concerned?
7. Have the rights of all potential resource persons within the school been anticipated and protected?
8. How will access to resource persons be controlled?
9. Have advance arrangements been made to secure the services of volunteer resource persons in the community? How has this been done? How are students advised?
10. Do all resource persons have an adequate understanding of the program and their potential role in it? Are they sympathetic and agreeable?
11. Is the program so structured that a major supervisory burden does *not* fall upon any resource person?
12. Is the school library the only place in the school where independent study may be conducted? Why?
13. Are students expected to develop independent study habits in the midst of general confusion? What are reasonable limits of tolerance in this matter? To what extent do school study conditions differ from those in the home? Should reasonable quiet prevail?
14. Are there places in the school that offer quiet study for those that need it?
15. What space and time inadequacies are predictable? Are they insurmountable, or can the program be built around them? How?

VI. THE PROCESSES OF RESPONSIBLY EVALUATING STU-
DENT AND PROGRAM STRENGTHS AND WEAKNESSES.

1. What pre-testing procedures will the program employ? What post-testing procedures?
2. Will the program have a self-evaluation system? How will it function? How will it be supervised?
3. What will be the relationship of evaluation to announced objectives?
4. Is there a grading policy? What is it?
5. Will the student have a voice in the grading? How?
6. How will the evaluation be reported to parents? To counselors?
7. Will an anecdotal record be kept? Who will keep it?
8. Will the evaluation be discussed with the student? How, when, and by whom?
9. How will feedback from the student and others be collected and processed? Will it be made part of the evaluation of the program?
10. Will the program itself be evaluated? How?
11. Will the service of the TPS Research Department be used? If not, why not?

VII. PROVISIONS FOR MODIFYING PROCESSES WHEN NECESSARY.

1. Will the student be permitted to drop the program without penalty? Permanently? Temporarily?
2. Is the program flexible enough so that radical changes may be made as needed? What procedures have been developed for any contingency that may arise?
3. Are student attitudes to be measured? How? Attitudinal changes?
4. Will student attitudes be allowed to modify objectives? Relationships?
5. Does the program recognize the student's need for rest and reassessment, that learning goes by fits and starts more than by constant orderly progression? How is this provided for?
6. What specific problems are imaginable in the implementation of this program? What solutions are possible?

VIII. Problems of Individualized Instruction — How Some Successful Programs Deal With Them

Dr. Sutton earned her Ph.D in Foreign-Language Education at Ohio State University and wrote her dissertation on individualized foreign-language instruction. She is a member of Kappa Delta Pi and Sigma Delta Pi. Dr. Sutton delivered one of the main addresses at the Conference on Individualized Instruction of Foreign Languages held at Stanford University in May, 1971.

INTRODUCTION

In the following article, Dr. Sutton provides an overview of typical problems encountered when implementing individualized foreign language instruction. Descriptions of several programs in practice are included, and hints toward the solution of these problems are offered.

The introduction of individualized instruction into a conventional foreign-language program cannot be done effectively and efficiently without allowing ample time to consider and analyze the changes in procedures, use of personnel, materials, equipment, available space, and the establishment of suitable educational goals. The roles of students and teachers are changed considerably; evaluations may be different even though a conventional grading system is still being used by the school; subject matter and a standardized text may no longer be the nucleus around which the course is constructed; and time needs to be disregarded as a measurement of students' achievements.

Pre-planning is essential. Unfortunately, it has been noted during observations in schools using individualized instruction, that in schools and programs where pre-planning and organization have not been carefully considered the results are often disappointing. Visitors to these programs are discouraged and disenchanted with the possibilities individualized instruction offers. Students and teachers are only confused when suddenly given freedom without sufficient direction, and inclined to interpret the new freedom as laxity. The exact opposite is true in schools where teachers, and often students, have planned carefully and anticipated some of the changes and the problems that could result from these changes.

In order to aid teachers in planning and organizing individualized foreign-language programs, a series of questions has been proposed that teachers may want to consider before beginning individualized foreign-language instruction in their schools. The questions, as the discussion of each that follows, are based on personal observations made during visits to schools engaged in some form of individualized foreign-language instruction, on information from a questionnaire sent to schools using individualized foreign-language instruction, from a questionnaire sent to a panel of authorities on foreign-language education, and on information found in the literature.[1]

It is extremely doubtful that there is any particular solution that can be considered "the" answer to any particular question, since individualized instruction is innately diversified in approach. The purpose of the questions and the discussion that follows each of them is to stimulate thinking and to act as guidelines for educators to analyze and interpret in terms of their own students, school, and community. Hopefully this chapter will enable teachers to begin their programs with greater understanding of some of the problems and issues that will be encountered. Perhaps those already engaged in some form of individualized instruction will find solutions to some of their problems and ideas worthy of use with their own students. In addition, perhaps teacher educators can utilize this synthesis of observations and current thinking about individualized foreign-language instruction to guide their future teachers in the successful use of individualized instruction.

------

[1] These four procedures were used to obtain information for "A Feasibility Study of Individualized Foreign Language Programs in the High Schools of the United States." Ph.D. Dissertation, The Ohio State University, 1971, written by this author. The questionnaires referred to and a complete tabulation of the results of these questionnaires, are presented in the dissertation.

Why Individualized Foreign-Language Instruction?

Throughout the foreign-language journals one encounters an insistence that greater consideration must be given to the individual[2] (Olmo, 1966; Sweet, 1968; Fearing, 1969; Strasheim, 1969). Instead of allowing only the "ideal" foreign-language student to enroll, many schools are now accepting and encouraging all interested students[3] (Remer, 1963; Parent, 1968; Reinert, 1970). Consequently, foreign-language teachers are finding that there is a much wider variation in the students' abilities to learn foreign languages and the students' reasons for wanting to learn a foreign language than when classes were restricted to students who were college-bound and who had demonstrated by their grades in other subjects that they were academically talented.

This situation presents an unprecedented challenge to the foreign-language classroom teacher who has been accustomed to teaching only the students who had proven ability to succeed in other subjects and who in the past could recommend that students who were unable to learn the conjugation of irregular verbs might well transfer to art, shop, or typing.

Coupled with the problem of making foreign-language study appeal to the new student in the classroom is the reduction or abolition of foreign-language requirements for high-school graduation and college entrance[4] (Kersten & Ott, 1970; Zeldner,

---

[2] See for example articles by: Guillermo del Olmo, "Individualized Instruction: The Classroom Situation," *Language Learning: The Individual and the Process*, ed. by Edward W. Najam and Carleton T. Hodge, *International Journal of American Linguistics*, XXXII, 1 part II (1966), 161–69; Waldo Sweet, "Integrating Other Media with Programmed Instruction," *The Modern Language Journal*, LII, 7 (November 1968), 420–23; Percy Fearing, "Non-graded Forieng Language Classes," *Foreign Language Annals*, II, 3 (March 1969), 343–47; and Lorraine A. Strasheim, "Where From Here?" *The Modern Language Journal*, LII, 7 (November 1969), 493–97.

[3] See for example articles by: Ilo Remer, *A Handbook for Guiding Students in Modern Foreign Languages* (Washington, D.C.: U.S. Printing Office, 1963); Paul P. Parent, "Minimizing Dropouts in the Foreign Language Program." *The Modern Language Journal*, LII, 4 (April 1968), 189–91; and Harry Reinert, "Student Attitudes Toward Foreign Language — No Sale!" *The Modern Language Journal*, LIV, 2 (February 1970), 107–12.

[4] See Caesar S. Kersten and Vesperella E. Ott, "How Relevant Is Your Foreign Language Program?" *The Modern Language Journal*, LIV, 1 (January 1970), 9–13; or Harry Reinert, "Student Attitudes Toward Foreign Language — No Sale!" *The Modern Language Journal*, LIV, 2 (February 1970), 107–12.

1966). This has brought to the attention of teachers the fact that they can no longer anticipate that a certain percentage of the high-school students will enroll in the college preparatory program and sign up for a foreign language class to satisfy requirements for graduation in a specific curriculum. This means that foreign languages will have to compete with every other elective for the students' time and preferences.

Many educators see individualized foreign-language instruction as the most feasible means of compensating for the students' wider variation of foreign-language learning abilities and the various reasons the students in today's foreign-language courses have for studying foreign language. Individualized instruction can be a means of giving students a more appealing and a more satisfactory foreign-language experience and may therefore encourage them to want to begin and continue foreign-language study. Administrators are looking favorably on attempts by their teachers to individualize instruction, not only because parents and students appear to prefer it to regular classroom instruction, but also because there are scattered reports that individualized instruction makes better and more efficient use of existing equipment and personnel, and is therefore more economical.

Other advantages will also become apparent in the suggested answers to other questions.

WHAT IS INDIVIDUALIZED INSTRUCTION?

In most literature a precise definition of individualized instruction is avoided. The reader is left to form his own opinion from clues given in the text as to how the program intends to compensate for individual differences, and which individual differences are to be given consideration. One definite attempt to define individualized instruction is by Altman[5] (1971). He says the usual definitions are true and accurate, and yet the classroom teacher has little information as to the practical classroom application of individualization of instruction.

Altman begins his definition with what it is not. He says it is not a "method;" it is not the same phenomenon as "do-your-own-thing;" it is not the same as independent study although independent study may be a part of individualized instruction;

[5] Howard B. Altman, "Toward a Definition of Individualized Foreign Language Instruction," *American Foreign Language Teacher*, III (February, 1971).

and it does not mean that the foreign-language teacher has to teach each student on a one-to-one basis all of the time.

His final definition has four parts:
(a) Each student is allowed to progress through his curriculum materials at his own pace;
(b) Each student is tested only when he is prepared to be tested (thus implying that not all students in a class will be tested simultaneously);
(c) When a student needs help, he works individually with his teacher, or with some other "resource person" in the classroom, in a tutorial manner; and
(d) Each student is aware of the nature of his learning task, and knows what he must demonstrate, and with what degree of accuracy he must demonstrate it, to receive credit for his work and to be able to move ahead in his materials. (ms.)

This definition assumes that there is a core of materials to be mastered by the student. Certainly there are educationally sound reasons for this type of individualization to be used in the beginning lessons, because there is a certain amount of basic vocabulary, syntax, and phonology that must be mastered before personally satisfying activities can be undertaken.

In a number of programs, individualization is more extensive, particularly after these basics are learned. Logan (1970) says, ". . . what is meant by individualization is subject to broad and varied interpretation."[6] To illustrate, he says:

> In some programs the individualization is a matter of the rate at which a student can learn a set course of study through which all students must progress; in others the individualization consists of the traditional "lock-step" operation with the individualization consisting of individual or small group help for students with specific problems in keeping up with the class; in other cases we find grouping based on common goals or similar aptitudes; in still other programs we find such approaches as tracking, team teaching, individual demand scheduling, ungraded learning centers, and independent study, including correspondence courses. More closely approaching true individualization are those programs offering individualized contracts to each

---

[6] Gerald E. Logan, "Curricula for Individualized Instruction," *Britannica Review of Foreign Language Education, Vol. II* (Chicago: Encyclopaedia Britannica, 1970).

student; sequential learning packets which can be combined for different students in different ways; or even essentially random learning approaches.[7] (pp. 1–2).

The above definitions serve to illustrate the wide variety of interpretations of individualized instruction as it is being practiced in the high schools in the United States today.

In an effort to define individualized instruction and study more precisely, a questionnaire was sent to leading authorities, both practitioners and theoreticians, in foreign-language education and related fields, in order to compose a jury for judging various aspects and concepts of individualized instruction. A list of forty names were selected from the literature available on individualized foreign-language instruction or related topics. From this list, Dr. Otto of The Ohio State University aided in the final selection of fifteen members. All are well known in the foreign-language profession or have published materials concerning some facet of individualized instruction during the past year. An attempt was also made to choose jurors who represented different positions in relationship to the actual teaching and the students in order to take advantage of their different perspectives.

Of the fifteen sent the questionnaire, eleven responded.[8] There are considerable differences in the opinions of the jurors. Some of this divergence is because of the way the questions were stated; some of the divergence is due to the wide variety of positions the jurors occupy in relationship to individualized foreign-language instruction; and perhaps some is because there really is no widespread agreement on what is meant by individualizing instruction or how it can be accomplished.

There were, however some areas of agreement which emerged. All considered certain characteristics essential, and many

---

[7] Ibid., pp. 1–2.

[8] Those responding to the questionnaire were: Howard B. Altman, Director of Foreign Language Interns, Stanford University; John B. Carroll, Senior Research Psychologist, Educational Testing Service; Marianne Ciotti, Assistant Professor, Department of Foreign Languages, Boston University; Juan Estarellas, Department of Modern Languages, Florida Atlantic University; Percy Fearing, Minnesota State Foreign Language Consultant; Ronald L. Gougher, Associate Professor of German, West Chester State College; Almon G. Hoye, Director, Marshall-University High School, Minneapolis, Minnesota; Fred LeLeike, Director of Individualized Study Project, West Bend High School, West Bend, Wisconsin; Theodore H. Mueller, Professor of French and Education, University of Kentucky; John Rallo, Department Chairman, Darien High School, Darien, Connecticut; Waldo Sweet, Professor of Latin and Teaching Latin, University of Michigan.

characteristics the majority would approve have been identified. From the jury's responses to this questionnaire it is possible to formulate acceptable guidelines for the establishment of individualized instruction with certain minimum specifications. The following are recommendations that the author has formulated from their responses.

Those answering the questionnaire concurred that *all* students should be permitted to take a foreign language, most choosing all students and a few choosing all motivated students. Their answers appeared to agree that an essential characteristic is that time should be flexible permitting each student to proceed at his own learning rate and pursue his individual interests, with extra time provided for those students who need it and provision for those who are able to move rapidly ahead, as possible or desired. The jurors have indicated that grouping procedures should be of the flexible type, where students may work alone or in different-sized groups depending on the activity in which the students are engaged and the student's ability or interest, and with movement from one group to another as the individual's interests or needs dictate. The reactions to students and teachers planning together indicated that the jurors are in favor of the student and teacher setting mutually acceptable goals and pacing accordingly. All of the members of the jury agreed or strongly agreed that the students should be measured by previously established goals for each unit; that the program should be able to provide records to guide students, parents, colleges, and prospective employers, as to the levels of proficiency attained; and that students should be kept aware of their progress. Most agreed that it is more important to learn smaller amounts of material well than to cover larger amounts of material.

Concerning materials, the majority of the respondents agreed with the finding in the literature that programmed learning may be used as a part of the total program and augmented by other types of instruction. Few educators today recommend that programmed learning be used as the total program except when the student is highly motivated and a teacher is not available.[9]

_____

[9] Waldo E. Sweet, "Integrating Other Media with Programmed Instruction." *The Modern Language Journal*, LII, 7 (November 1968), 420–23; and Douglas Porter, "A Report on Instructional Devices in Foreign Language Teaching." *Teaching Machines and Programmed Learning: A Source Book.* Ed. by Arthur A. Lumsdaine and Robert Glaser (National Education Association, 1960), 186–205.

(See for example, Sweet, 1968 or Porter, 1960.) Existing texts divided into packets or units, remedial materials and enrichment materials combined with a wide variety of media may be used.

The jurors concurred that a good program is flexible and provides for individual differences in learning rates, abilities, and various individual goals. Evidences of a good program are: the number of students who want to continue foreign-language study; and teachers' estimations of how effectively they are able to provide for students' characteristics.

The responses to these items do not indicate a particular type of individualized instruction as being preferable, but they do indicate some characteristics good programs should have. This presents the flexibility of interpretation that is needed in an area as new and personalized as individualized instruction. This also indicates that individualized instruction can be accomplished by employing many different approaches, devices, and arrangements. For these reasons, definitions and characteristics describing individualized instruction are almost of necessity varied and depending upon one's perspective.

WHAT INDIVIDUAL DIFFERENCES THAT INFLUENCE STUDENTS' LEARNING PROGRESS NEED TO BE TAKEN INTO CONSIDERATION?

First of all, there are many variations of learning characteristics that students bring to the learning situation. Bloom (1969) has identified the variables as: aptitude for particular kinds of learning, ability to understand instruction and perseverance, which in turn are affected by the quality of instruction and the time allowed for learning.[10] Reynolds (1963) brings out the idea that students differ in the ways they learn, as well as in ability, with his question, "Which method is better for whom?" Pimsleur, Sundland, and McIntyre (1966) have identified the lack of auditory discrimination ability and the lack of continuity in teaching and learning as important reasons students of all abilities may find studying foreign language a frustrating experience.[11] (In many individualized instructional programs,

---

[10] Benjamin S. Bloom, "Learning for Mastery," *UCLA Evaluation Comment*, I, 2 (Los Angeles, 1968), 17–19.

[11] Paul Pimsleur, Donald M. Sundland, and Ruth D. McIntyre, *Under-Achievement in Foreign Language Learning.* (New York: The Modern Language Association of America, 1966.)

continuity and sequencing are not a problem, even for transfer students.)

There are variations resulting from motivation and interest. Nelson and Jakobovits (1970) have identified the student's sense of accomplishment as a motivating factor, and as a result suggest that ". . . (teachers) offer courses that teach specific goals in which the student is interested (so that perseverance and motivation come from within and are not externally imposed)."[12] Rivers (1964) considers the individual's levels of aspiration as also an important consideration of individual differences.[13] (p. 59). Carroll (1968) states that learner characteristics are inhibited or enhanced by classroom management and places importance on the way teachers organize materials and utilize time, in addition to the ways students utilize their own time.[14] Carroll (1968) defines aptitude as the amount of learning time (not to be confused with elapsed time which includes such activities as sitting at the desk dreaming, wasting time, and so forth), under the best teaching conditions, it takes a student to learn to perform a task that he could not perform before or understand a concept previously not understood.[15] Therefore, the shorter the learning time required, the higher the inferred aptitude. Programmed learning experiments have shown that there is a wide variation in the amount of time different students take to achieve the same degree of mastery.[16] (See Carroll, 1966; Clark and Clark, 1966; Valdman, 1964.) Experiments have also shown the student has a greater "survival" rate when he is

---

[12] Robert J. Nelson and Leon A. Jakobovits, eds. "Motivation in Foreign Language Learning." *Northeast Conference on the Teaching of Foreign Languages, 1970.*

[13] Wilga Rivers, *The Psychologist and the Foreign Language Teacher* (Chicago: The University of Chicago Press, 1964), p. 59.

[14] John B. Carroll, "Memorandum: On Needed Research in the Psycholinguistic and Applied Psycholinguistic Aspects of Language Teaching." *Foreign Language Annals,* I, 3 (March 1968), 236–38.

[15] Ibid.

[16] See for examples articles by John B. Carroll, "Individual Differences in Foreign Language Learning." *Proceedings: Thirty-Second Annual Foreign Language Conference at New York University.* Ed. by Marvin Wasserman (New York: New York University School of Education, Division of Foreign Language and International Relations Education, 1966), 3–11; William H. Clark and Margaret G. Clark, "Achievement in Elementary German under Programmed and Conventional Instruction: A Preliminary Study," *The Modern Language Journal,* L, 2 (February 1966), 97–100; Albert Valdman, "Toward Self-Instruction in Foreign Language Learning," *International Review of American Linguistics,* II (1964), 1–36.

allowed to progress through the materials at his own rate.[17] (Adams, E. N., et al., 1968; Adams, C., 1967; Boyd-Bowman, 1966; Mueller, 1968.)

Teachers contemplating the use of individualized foreign-language instruction may want to expand these concepts to take into consideration social factors which affect their students' learning, such as one's family expectation, one's self expectation, one's value system and the value system of one's peer group, membership to a particular ethnic group, or one's economic or social position.

WHAT TRENDS AND PRACTICES IN INDIVIDUALIZED STUDY PROGRAMS SHOW THE MOST PROMISE?

It should be noted that the majority of individualized foreign-language programs are relatively new. There is still a great deal to be learned as more and more programs are begun and as teachers report their experiences and practices. The schools visited, the teachers using individualized instruction who were corresponded with, and the programs presented in the literature are making genuinely commendable efforts to provide for individual differences. The teachers conducting individualized instructional programs are using a wide variety of techniques and approaches to individual differences and interests which agree with many of the guidelines for good programs as identified by the jurors.

Schools of all sizes are engaged in some type of individualized instruction, from schools of less than 500 pupils to schools of over 3,000 pupils. The schools are located in a variety of geographic areas, from large metropolitan areas to small rural communities. All possible grouping combinations are used, and many combinations of re-grouping techniques are found within the initial framework. The programs are using many types of instructional media, and again many combinations that appeal

---

[17] See for examples articles by E. N. Adams, H. W. Morrison, J. M. Reddy, "Conversation with a Computer as a Technique of Language Instruction." *The Modern Language Journal,* LII, 1 (January, 1968), 3–16; Charles L. Adams, "Independence for Study," *Hispania,* L, 3 (September, 1967), 483–87; or Peter Boyd-Bowman, "Self-Instruction in the 'Neglected' Languages: A Progress Report from Kalamazoo College," *The Modern Language Journal,* L, 1 (January, 1966), 21–23; and Theodore Mueller, "Programmed Instruction: Help for the Linguistically 'Underprivileged'," *The Modern Language Journal,* LII, 2 (February, 1968), 79–84.

to individual differences, preferences, and interests. Basic materials are often supplemented with other media, programmed materials, a variety of texts, and resources, including resource persons who may come from other departments in the school or from the community.

A few programs will be reviewed in some detail in order to illustrate some of the practices and innovations that have proven successful to these schools and because these schools are solving problems in a practical way that seem to confront those beginning individualization. These programs represent approaches of different types of individualized instruction. There are other equally noteworthy programs in progress. A list of articles in the literature describing additional programs follows this article, with the hope that teachers and schools interested in implementing some form of individualized instruction will find it helpful to consult these articles during their initial planning.

Freedom High School
Bethlehem, Pennsylvania

At Bethlehem, Pennsylvania, under the direction of Mr. Robert Worsley, the program is in its second year. Ronald L. Gougher, a member of the panel of authorities, was program consultant on the project. In order to bring recognition and acceptance to the values of individualized instruction, Gougher is concentrating on using students who have demonstrated above-average classroom ability during the first year of language study. The following year, these students are put in a seminar situation where they do all of the regular classroom assignments, and in addition have a variety of enrichment activities and materials at their disposal. Students are allowed to use these materials at their own rate. Since students are all above average in ability and motivation, they usually complete much more than would be expected in the classroom. Exactly how much more varies a great deal even among these select students.

The students meet with the instructor first during each scheduled class period, for announcements, questions, and possible directions. After a few minutes, they are permitted to go to the seminar room adjacent to the library or remain in the small meeting room to work on materials that do not require special equipment. Students may also use the seminar room during any of their study periods, or other free time, and do so from three to five periods a week. All students are given the standard texts, readers, and programs used in the Bethlehem Area School District. In addition to these materials, the students have at their disposal an audio-lingual grammar, a grammar-oriented workbook, additional readers, a college grammar summary, a book on how to take college board tests, a variety of tapes and testing materials, records, filmstrips, and movies. The students work with these materials together, alone, or with the help of the instructor.

Discipline problems are virtually non-existent. Students can be placed in the regular classroom if their temperaments prove unsuitable for the expected assumption of responsibility. Other than a little extraneous talking, the majority apply themselves diligently to their tasks. The standards and goals of the program are kept high. All students involved understand that they will be encouraged and helped whenever necessary.

The amount of work covered has improved both in quantity and in quality. All of the students are at least a half a year ahead, and some have gone considerably further, in the materials as well as displayed competence in the language. All students involved thus far have received "A," regardless of the amount of work completed, because all would have received "A" if they had been in a regular class. These students do not receive extra credit or recognition. Their rewards are their own personal satisfaction and a letter covering their performance and level completed becomes a part of their permanent record. The students' scholastic accomplishments have been demonstrated by all receiving 600+ on the Educational Testing Service College Board Tests. In addition, in the yearly tests conducted by the American Association of Teachers of German, one Freedom High Student placed second in the third-year category, and three students took all first three places in the second-year category.

The goals of this program are conventional—fulfilling high-school and college requirements. However, the program is promising because it shows what can be done with above-average students, who are not necessarily brighter than students found in most other schools. These students are able to achieve above-average results with average efforts. Hopefully, the results will be generalized to what will be the results for average and below-average students in programs that admit all students to individualized foreign language.

Bates Junior High School
Annapolis, Maryland

The program at Bates Junior High School, a Multi-Media Project makes use of video tapes, audio tapes, written programmed materials, transparencies, sketches, and illustrations. All of the materials have been constructed and executed by the members of the project. The program in its present state is considered semi-final because it is constantly being revised and validated with classes.

The student's progress is measured by precise behavioral objectives for each unit, which are called Terminal Objective (T.O.) Blocks. A student may take a pre-test, and if the pre-test shows that he already possesses the criterion behavior, he proceeds immediately to the next T.O. Block for which he has entry behavior. A student selects his route from a group of T.O. Blocks for which he has the necessary entering behavior and which are selected from a flow chart posted for the students. A student may not attempt a T.O. Block until he has completed the entry behavior for it. He does not leave the T.O. Block until he has met the criteria set forth in the objectives, although he may vary his efforts meanwhile with other T.O. Blocks for which he does have the entry behavior. The teacher monitors each student's completion of a T.O. Block. The student must give evidence of being able to perform the behavior prescribed for by the terminal objectives of the unit; however, it is frequently possible to evaluate the performance of a small group rather than examine each student individually. Branches are available for remedial help, enrichment, reinforcement, and additional practice.

The area used by the program consists of two adjoining large classrooms. The desks have been removed and replaced by small tables that can be joined to make larger tables in a variety of shapes. The rooms have been carpeted, and acoustical ceilings have been installed. The equipment is all about the rooms. Work areas can be enlarged or moved when it is necessary. Study carrels have electrical outlets, so that any of the electronic equipment can be utilized in them. All kinds of equipment are available. All of the materials, including the T.O. Blocks and the student progress sheets, are stored where the students can locate them and use them, thus eliminating the need of anyone spending time or effort dispensing materials. Students also assume the responsibility for the replacement of materials when their work is completed.

Some of the students work in groups; others work alone. Grouping arrangements depend entirely on the activity students are engaged in; however, the large-group arrangement is seldom used after the initial introduction to the course. Two classes are scheduled to the rooms at the same time. Students move freely from room to room.

The materials in this case form another type of lock-step arrangement; however, the students have the choice of many routes to achieve the goals of the program and can proceed through the materials at their own rates.

While visiting the program, an outstanding video tape, teaching French phonology, was observed. It seemed practical, both timewise and moneywise, to present phonology on tape. The teacher checks and re-directs the students almost immediately following their viewing of the tape, thus there is little danger of students learning faulty pronunciation during individual practice. The students could both see and hear the video tape better than in a classroom situation. This process frees the teacher from endless repetition for class after class. Teachers need to free themselves from activities that can be done as well or better by machines.

The original cost of the program was high; the major expenses were the cost of the equipment and the employment of staff during two summers to construct the program, make the tapes, both video and audio, and devise T.O. Blocks.

Marshall-University High School
Minneapolis, Minnesota

(See a detailed description written by the director of this program in Chapter IX of this volume.)

At Marshall-University High School, German, I, II, III, and French II are completely individualized. All of the other classes are individualized fifty percent or more. In addition, "Mini-Courses" are offered on an elective basis for students who have completed the basic-skills language courses. The "Mini-Courses" appeal to a variety of student interests and long-term needs. They attempt to give as many students as possible a successful and meaningful experience in foreign-language learning.

Students have had a voice in preparing the "Mini-Courses." The staff devoted class time to general discussion. Career possibilities were explored along with their accompanying linguistic competencies. Leisure-time activities were also discussed as they relate to language knowledge. From these discussions, titles for over one hundred short courses were listed and from this list approximately fifty titles have been developed into program offerings in French, German, Spanish, and Russian.

The program is completely flexible. Students with busy schedules may drop foreign language and enroll in "Mini-Courses" from time to time, thus maintaining their skills. Students with unusual interest may take more than one course at the same time, or enroll in another foreign language while continuing studying the first language on a more limited basis. Students with academic interests may register for courses in grammar, composition, history, or culture. Those planning a career in business might choose conversation, letter writing, or a travel course.

An interesting aspect of the program is the school's gradual transition from a standard schedule to flexible scheduling. During the interim a modified modular schedule was used. Although this allowed for a great deal of flexibility, the foreign-language staff and students were begging for more flexible use of time in order to have suitable scheduling for the "Mini-Courses." This prevented the usual confusion that accompanies the swift change from a standard schedule to a completely flexible schedule. Both students and teachers were anxiously awaiting flexible scheduling because there was an existing need for it.

All of the foreign-language facilities are grouped. The regular classrooms are in the same corridor; there is a teachers' office where joint planning and conferences may take place and an adjoining laboratory and resource center. Students assigned to the classrooms may either work there or go to the resource center. Students may work alone, in small groups, or on independent study. Some students, who are unable to schedule a regular class, work completely alone during their free time and confer with the teachers on a regular basis. Most of the major textbook series are available to the students, as well as a variety of laboratory equipment.

Students at Marshall-University High School enjoy foreign-language study; even students who would be considered academically slow continue to study foreign language. The language laboratory is unattended and this has not presented a problem. Students are also better satisfied because they are consulted as to where and what they will study. All students with varying abilities and interest are admitted and benefitting from foreign-language study. Time is not a limiting factor because facilities

54010

are always available and students are not expected to reach a pre-determined level by a certain time. Grouping is according to activity and students may join one group or another as their interests and needs change.

Central Junior High School
Greenwich, Connecticut

At Central Junior High School, another type of program is encountered that is flourishing across the country because so few changes are necessary. It is individualized foreign-language instruction carried on within the confines of the ordinary classroom, within a seven-period day. This of course means that any teacher who desires to individualize may do so under these circumstances.

The classroom has been completely rearranged. Around the outside are tables with equipment. Tables hold tape recorders, cassette recorders, language masters, record players, and an overhead projector. Along the wall too are study carrels for individual work, and storage for materials which are all at the disposal of the students. A large file cabinet holds the materials for the continuous progress units, transparencies for the overhead projector, worksheets with a master key for examination preparation; tapes, cassettes, and other materials are on shelves readily available to the students. In the center of the room are two round tables for group work.

At the center of the program is a conventional text, divided and amplified to give students an opportunity to find remedial work that is appropriate to their level if it is needed; and to allow students to skip sections of added drill if they are prepared to move ahead.

Even a program of such limited scope has created very favorable results. There has been no increase in cost. Although more effort is expended by everyone, students included, the students' attitude towards foreign-language study is favorable, which is not only expressed in their active participation, but also in the reduction of the dropout rate.

Mountain View High School
Cupertino, California

Robert McLennan at Mountain View High School has completely individualized the German program within a system of modular scheduling, without the use of more than one classroom.

His classroom is arranged similar to the one above. An unconventional addition is a conversation area, complete with a couch, which has added an atmosphere of informality. Here, students display to the teacher the knowledge they have learned elsewhere in the room with the use of electronic equipment, from the reading materials, from one another and with the teacher aide. This program also uses a conventional text divided into units. The student receives a check list of activities to which he must conform to complete a chapter of work. This includes listening, speaking, reading, and writing skills. As the student completes the work, he is tested immediately and must achieve a minimum proficiency level before he is allowed to continue. If the student does not display minimum proficiency, his efforts are re-directed to bring his performance up to a level suitable for continuation.

McLennan reports that there has been a remarkable change in the students' attitudes. Students respond well to being allowed to move at a pace which is commensurate with their ability. Attrition has been greatly reduced. Placement for new students is no longer a problem. The conversations are informal and relevant to the students.

McLennan has some excellent suggestions for teachers who feel overwhelmed with the added duties of individualization. Students can file student papers and tests; help keep attendance records for conversation groups; give and correct quizzes or dictations; help students in lower phases do workbook and oral exercises; help regulate electronic equipment; keep the room neat; help maintain a German atmosphere in the Language Island.

In addition to student helpers, McLennan uses German-Speaking members of the community, or people in the community who have traveled to German-speaking countries, to bring the students enriched experiences. He encourages the "German" visitors to be German, shake hands, gesture, wear costumes if they like, and the visitors are encouraged to present or teach a song, dance, poem; as well as speak the language and display pictures, slides or realia.

Live Oak High School
Morgan Hill, California

Gerald Logan at Live Oak High School has found the solution to scheduling. Instead of offering five levels of German during separate periods, all levels of German are offered every period of every day.

During the first two levels of foreign-language study, while the basics of phonology, vocabulary, and syntax are being learned, the individualization is mainly a matter of rate of speed. Students are permitted to learn as much as they wish, or as slowly as may be necessary.

After the first two levels have been completed, the individualization consists of content as well as quantity. The content is tailored to the students' future plans and interests, whether they may be college, vocational, travel, or simply pleasure.

Each student has an individual file where both the student and teacher can note this progress. Each student is evaluated separately, even though students with similar abilities or interests may be grouped to work on materials together. Large groups are formed from time to time to view movies, sing, or discuss various aspects of Germany.

Some of the advantages Logan has found are that by students learning at their own rates and with materials that are relevant to each student's personality, motivation is increased. The problems of scheduling are eliminated. The school can offer a particular "course" even if only one student is interested in it. Articulation problems are nonexistent either for students within the program or for students entering from the eighth grade or from another school. Oral and written testing is done by the teacher, and thus a truly thorough and professional diagnosis and prescription for future study can be given.

With all of these advantages, there has been no increase in instructional costs. Two instructors have 230 students enrolled in this program. Logan says, "As enrollment grows and the programs are better developed, we see the teacher-pupil ratio decreasing markedly over the traditional ratio with no decrease in the quality of instruction." (mimeo.)

Hyde Park High School
Chicago, Illinois

Enid L. Turner at Hyde Park High School reports that, in 1966, students already enrolled in one language were given the opportunity to sample, on an independent study basis, any of the other modern languages offered by the school, French, German, Spanish, or Russian. Italian was offered through the use of individual study material and a professor from Chicago City College who came once a week and gave the students additional practice in Italian. In 1967, Japanese was added; in 1968, Hausa, an African language, was added. Beginning in 1968, all foreign-language independent study courses were made non-credit and opened to all interested students, whether they had previously had a language, or had been considered academically "ready or capable" of enrolling in a foreign-language course. Students may enter or withdraw at any time, since it is purely a voluntary program.

University of Colorado Program for Small High Schools

An interesting program representing one of the possible uses of individualized instruction, is being conducted from the University of Colorado, under the direction of David F. Mercer.[18] The program brings foreign-language study to small schools (less than 500 students) and those which cannot afford a language teacher or language laboratory equipment.

Spanish, Levels I and II, are offered through the university with the use of texts, workbooks, video tapes, audio tapes, and telelectures (amplified telephone). The schools need to supply a supervisor to oversee the program and the use of equipment consisting of video tape recorder and monitor, a magnetic tape recorder, and a 16-mm sound movie projector, all of which may be rented or purchased. Once a week, there is also a telelecture (by amplified telephone installed by the telephone company) where students can ask questions and the university personnel can check on the students' progress.

Individual differences in ability to learn foreign languages are taken into account by allowing faster students to proceed at their own pace through independent study, with slower students working as rapidly as ability permits and through extra work in individual study. The total cost is about $1900 for both levels and $45 per student the first year. When the costs are compared with the cost of a teacher, classroom, materials and equipment needed for a foreign-language program, they are relatively small. Students tested in the Spring of 1971 did as well or better

---

[18] David F. Mercer, "A Comparison of Standard Classroom and Correspondence Study Instruction in First Year High School Spanish." Doctoral Dissertation University of Wisconsin, 1971.

than students in a regular classroom. The program is now being enlarged to include French.

This program could serve as a model and as a possible approach to permitting the teaching of languages not commonly offered in high schools. Furthermore, there are still many states in the United States that have a large number of small high schools, such as Alaska, the mountain states, and the plains states.

All of the programs are overcoming obstacles that possibly could have been allowed to be restricting. Teachers have been able to find materials that are suitable for their students' interests and abilities by adapting conventional texts to their students' needs, by dividing them into packets or units, and by using programmed, enrichment, and remedial materials as a part of the total program. Scheduling restrictions are being overcome by making facilities available to students during times other than during their regular scheduled class periods. The different amounts of time needed for learning by individuals is being adjusted by permitting students to progress through materials at their own learning rates. Different grouping arrangements are being used, depending on the activities of the students. Many programs allow students to engage in independent study by having the student sign a written contract, after the student and teacher have agreed upon a suitable goal, the means for achieving it, and a time limit. A wide variety of means of presentation is being used by these programs: books, workbooks, periodicals, as well as a wide variety of electronic means of presentation such as video tape recorders, 8-mm and 16-mm film projectors, language laboratories, tape recorders, overhead projectors, and language masters.

These programs which have been reported also indicate that the students gain a great deal under individualized instruction. Most of these schools, and in all cases where the question was specifically asked, have indicated that fewer discipline problems are encountered. All of the above practices are likely to produce more satisfied students — students who will have more favorable attitudes toward foreign-language study. It also appears possible that these students may learn more subject matter, both because they are inclined to stay with foreign-language study longer, and because academically talented and interested students can move through the materials faster than the conventional levels that have been used to measure a year of foreign-language study.

WHAT ORGANIZATIONAL FEATURES, SUCH AS CLASS TIME, GRADES, CREDITS, COLLEGE ENTRANCE EXAMS, AND SO FORTH, ARE IMPOSING UNWARRANTED RESTRICTION UPON STUDENTS AND TEACHERS?

While the item itself did not appear in the questionnaire sent to the panel of authorities on foreign-language education or individualized instruction, the jurors indicated that time should not be used as a criterion for judgment of a student's ability. They also indicated that a program should be able to produce records to give colleges and prospective employers an indication of the proficiency levels attained. This further implies that some kind of criteria-referenced testing or proficiency rating scales will need to replace the Carnegie credit system. Anyone who has worked with second-year college students who were placed there because they had had two years of high-school foreign language someplace, taught by someone, can verify that the present system is unreliable and that achievement and proper levels of learning could be determined better by testing and proficiency ratings. In fact, most colleges have resorted to some type of placement testing because of the vast differences students have displayed in their knowledge and skills in foreign language.

A review of the literature and current observations validate that generally today all students, with the full gamut of academic abilities, are admitted to foreign-language classes, including many students who are not college bound. In all probability there will be an increased effort to attract students who are not necessarily college bound as requirements are lowered and abolished. This not only implies that students may not be academically as capable, but also that they may have interests not usually recognized in the design of traditional programs. Mundane happenings at the school or in the foreign country compared to their own circumstances are of more interest and value to these students than the architecture of Notre Dame, the style of Picasso, or the political development of Germany. Thus, the goals and values of foreign-language study need to be re-examined and adjusted to the occupants of today's foreign-language classes.

Organizational features have been overcome by a number of the schools engaged in individualizing foreign-language instruction. Time needs to be made more flexible, and today this is being done by simply making the rooms and facilities more available to students during their free periods, and by ceasing to evaluate students in terms of time criteria. Grades have not presented too great a problem because the parents, in most cases, are still seeing rather conventional grades given, and do not realize these may represent something different from the traditional. Most schools have indicated that they are not worrying about producing credits for colleges because so many colleges today do their own testing and placing anyway. In all cases where the question was asked, this is the way the problem is being handled. The program designers and teachers are solving the problems of grades, credits, and college entrance exams by refusing to let these mechanistic matters hamper or regulate their programs and by using some kind of equivalent to the traditional grading system.

WHAT ARE THE PROBLEMS OF EFFICIENT RECORD KEEPING?

Record keeping proves not to be the problem many anticipated it to be. According to the questionnaire sent to high schools using individualized instruction, some difficulties are indicated by beginning programs, but most of the schools are able to cope with the situation some time between the second and third years. The teachers are managing by letting students keep their own daily progress records, and the instructor records only his own personal final evaluation, on such things as unit tests, conversations in small groups, and in personal conversations. Usually each student has a separate file where he records the work he has completed. One program uses different colors of paper to indicate the type of work done. Teachers can verify the students' records by their own evaluations.

WHAT MATERIALS AND EQUIPMENT ARE BEING USED? WHAT MATERIALS AND EQUIPMENT ARE STILL NEEDED?

Materials particularly are in short supply. Most of the schools are adapting texts to their needs. Since so many of the programs have indicated good success with dividing current texts, it is suggested that textbook manufacturers revise their texts to the types of units and packets being used by these programs, as an expedient measure, and then begin working on the production of basic materials suitable for individualized study. The literature and jurors agree that programmed learning can make up a significant part of the total program. Fiks' (1969) list of available programmed materials should be examined for possible use.[19] Some are very suitable as supplements to teacher instruction; others are reasonably suitable for use as total instruction where a teacher is not available and the student is highly motivated. There is still a great need for good programs for language completely self-taught. Several have suggested that programs especially designed for individualized instruction would take the form of modified programmed materials, that are supplemented with other types of instruction supplied by the teacher, an aide, or the variety of media available. This does not presuppose that the materials need to be presented by expensive machines, but opens the possibility that programmed workbooks, films, tapes, and materials that can be integrated and used in ordinary schoolrooms would be suitable for individualized instruction. The schools have often requested materials that present a single grammar point or concept as one possibility of the shape these materials would take—packaged perhaps as the "single concept film loop."

No one has requested equipment that is not available on the market today. Whether this is due to lack of imagination or not is another matter. A number have suggested that equipment they would prefer is not within their school's budget.

One relatively inexpensive source of supplemental material is periodicals direct from the foreign country. Magazines, newspapers, travel folders, and so forth, printed in the country of the target language have authenticity, immediacy, and integrate current culture into foreign-language learning.

HOW MUCH DO THE VARIOUS INDIVIDUALIZED STUDY PROGRAMS COST BOTH IN DOLLARS AND STAFF TIME?

Pre-planning and organization seem to be very essential not only for a successful individualized study program but also for the most economical use of personnel, means, and materials. In almost all cases, teachers have indicated a need for more time to plan and direct individualized study programs. With better techniques being demonstrated and written about, teachers will not need to spend as much time trying to be creative. This is indeed a difficult task for teachers who were never trained to be textbook writers or program designers.

---

[19] A. I. Fiks, *Foreign Language Programmed Materials: 1969* (New York: MLA Materials Center, 1969).

Frequently it has been noted that teachers have not really freed themselves from many of the routine duties that students can do for themselves. Before beginning individualized instruction, the division of teacher responsibilities and student responsibilities should be an important part of the planning. An effective division of labor can, it is believed, actually save a school system money. Teacher time, when compared to paraprofessional time or the price of a few tapes, films, and equipment, is expensive. The initial outlay may be more than buying a text for each student, but when the expenses for the program are amortized over a period of years, for example five to ten years, the savings should appear.

Most of the programs examined cost about the same amount as regular classroom instruction, or a little more. Where the costs were much greater, it was because of the extra time personnel were hired to create and write the program. This procedure is not recommended, not only because of the expense, but also because most teachers do not have the necessary skills and knowledge needed for preparing these highly specialized materials. Adaptation and utilization of a variety of existing materials is much more feasible for most schools even now.

WHAT MEANS FOR EVALUATING STUDENTS AND PROGRAMS ARE VALID?

Goals are very important to both students and teachers engaged in individualized learning, because goals are the basic guidelines for the activities students will engage in and teachers will direct. The goals of individual students may be very different than they were when all of the students in the foreign-language program were studying foreign language in order to prepare for college. Previously, the usual goals of a foreign-language program, regardless of some rather vaguely stated extraneous objectives, such as to widen the cultural horizons of students, or to improve their English, were to teach the subject matter as presented in a particular text. The individual teacher's personal goal might read something like this: "Cover the first ten chapters by Christmas vacation and the remainder of the book by the end of school."

Teachers using individualized instruction are faced with pluralistic goals, interests, motives, abilities, and the social and psychological factors that influence their classes. The individual student's goals need to be carefully analyzed by the teacher, and it is the duty of the teacher to help the student both to establish a suitable goal and to achieve it. Short-range goals are important.

Students need to frequently feel the sense of accomplishment that achievement of a goal gives them. Long-range goals can be either made at the beginning for foreign-language study or deferred until later as the student progresses and sees what opportunities are available. Both the questionnaires sent to the jurors and the questionnaires sent to the schools engaged in individualized instruction indicated that it is preferable for students and teachers to plan together in order to establish suitable goals and means for achieving them.

In view of the fact that students studying foreign language today have varied abilities and varied interests, the usual judgements of a good program by the amount of subject matter covered by the students seems unsatisfactory. In fact, there is little previous precedent set that offers reliable measurements. Many current testing measures do not reflect the diversified goals of the programs. The jurors indicated that possible criteria for judgment of a good program include the increased numbers of students who want to continue foreign-language study and the teacher's judgments that they are providing better for the needs, desires, and interests of their students. These and related impressions show that the affective domain could and should figure in measuring the success of a student or program. From this information it seems just as logical to administer an attitude survey as a standardized achievement test to students in individualized study programs.

The issue cannot be avoided, or passed off easily. One of the points the jurors indicated strong agreement on was that a program should be able to provide students, parents, colleges, or future employers a measurement of the proficiency levels attained. This implies that some type of criterion-referenced testing, as recommended by Valette (1970), needs to be used.[20] If the time criterion or Carnegie credit system is to be abolished, certainly some type of suitable measurement needs to replace it.

TO WHAT EXTENT ARE TEACHERS ABLE TO ADJUST TO NEW ROUTINES AND PRACTICES IN ORDER TO CONDUCT INDIVIDUALIZED STUDY PROGRAMS EFFECTIVELY?

The jurors' greatest concern regarding the feasibility of individualized study today was the ability of teachers to adjust to the

---

[20] Rebecca Valette, "Teaching to Specific Objectives and Using Tests to Determine What Students Have Actually Mastered," an address delivered at the Oregon State Foreign Language Conference, October 9–10, 1970.

new routines and practices. Teachers, as students, need to proceed only after careful planning and organization in order not to have feelings of frustration because of lack of direction. It is a human trait to fear the unknown and consequently avoid it. It seems unrealistic to expect the majority of teachers to be sufficiently creative to originate practical patterns without realistic suggestions and time enough to internalize the new ideas and procedures. It is not unrealistic to expect many teachers to be able to follow proven and well presented suggestions and to be creative in their own way in their handling of organization within their own schools. Means already devised need to be demonstrated to teachers so that they know how to incorporate practices into their classes. Articles in journals can aid in the dissemination of useful ideas, and visiting good individualized programs, even in other fields, can be enlightening.

It seems preferable that all teachers to be involved in the program should have a part in the planning. New teachers can be screened and selected by their probable ability to adjust to these unorthodox procedures. Many of the programs now in progress use team teaching and/or a differentiated staff. This means that teachers need to cooperate and compromise with others. Some teachers accustomed to autonomous control of their own classrooms find this difficult. Having a voice in the planning and the assignment of a particular responsibility often helps to ease this tension.

Some division of labor is an essential element of individualized instruction. A careful analysis of what tasks can best be done by students, by para-professionals, or by teachers, leads to the best utilization of time.[21] Whether this analysis takes the form of a more formal system analysis with input and output diagrams or an informal round-table discussion with students, teachers, and administrators is of little consequence. What is really necessary is a planned and coordinated course of action that leads to mutually acceptable goals.

The use of a differentiated staff can be helpful and more economical. Teachers need time to teach. The use of teachers to take attendance, supervise activities, such as study halls, laboratories, and cafetarias, to do filing, typing, duplicating, and

---

[21] For helpful suggestions about activities that can be removed from the classroom see Florence Steiner, "Performance Objectives in the Teaching of Foreign Languages," *Foreign Language Annuals,* III (May 1970), 579–91.

other secretarial duties, is not economical and worse — oftentimes damaging to the interpersonal relationships teachers should have with their students. Teachers who have to assume the authoritarian role while on cafeteria duty or during study hall well know that there are times when the get-tough attitude seems to be the only way of maintaining order. This can prove to be damaging to the teacher's image as a classroom facilitator of learning. Assuming these added burdens can also drain teachers' creative energies, and impose unwarranted restriction on their teaching capabilities.

Asking the question, what roles does the teacher now assume that can be handled as well or better by other personnel, by machines, or by students, will lead to a division of labor that enables foreign-language programs to function not only more effectively and more efficiently, but more economically. Under conditions of individualized instruction, teachers need time to locate and to arrange materials suitable for each individual, to confer with students, to prepare for and evaluate individual's progress, as well as time to meet with large and small groups. Teachers need time to take into consideration the many individual differences of their students and the social and psychological factors involved in class interaction.

From available information, it is difficult to make a definite assessment of how well teachers are able to adjust to the new routines and practices. For the most part, the feasibility study reports only on schools using individualized instruction successfully. However, in some schools visited it was observed that some teachers, freed from the rigors of classroom attendance, spent too much time in the lounge instead of supervising and directing the learning activities of the students. An effort was made to contact schools no longer using individualized foreign-language instruction, which proved to be practically impossible. In the very few situations that were identified, the dropping of the plan resulted when the teacher who was using it left, or the administrator who supported the program was now in a different position. These findings indicate that the teacher or the administrator who supports the program is the real key to a successful program.

A complete re-education of teachers, such as in the attempts to convert teachers to audio-lingual techniques, is not needed. Teachers were reluctant to use these techniques because they themselves did not possess listening and speaking skills. Hence, they were hesitant to try to teach something they could not do themselves. The adjustment to individualizing instruction is easier and less threatening for teachers, partially because individualization can be begun gradually and increased as teachers and students adjust to the new routines and practices, and partially because many of the techniques are familiar to teachers. Many were taught this way in the grades, particularly in reading classes; many were exposed to the ideas in college; and many have been using similar approaches with their combined third- and fourth-year classes, to bring low achievers up to level and to give enrichment. With some commitment to improvement, well developed manuals, some available materials, and reasonable support and encouragement, many teachers should be able to move readily in the direction of individualizing instruction in foreign languages. Following the adage that, "Teachers teach as they were taught," teacher educators can facilitate the adoption of the different techniques by using individualized instruction with their students.

Anyone dedicated to the concept of individualized instruction can begin tomorrow to make plans. Behind every program visited and the majority of the programs reporting using individualized instruction, it was found that there was one person who was enthusiastic and supplying the vitality to make individualized instruction possible. Other faculty members follow the lead and augment the initial suggestions. It should not be overlooked, also, that some individualized instruction is being conducted by individuals in their own classrooms within the restrictions and confines of the physical facilities and organizational frameworks of their schools and other foreign-language programs in the school. It seems the only absolutely necessary ingredients to individualized instruction are an enthusiastic, creative person to supply the added ideas and energy needed and the permission to do so from either the department head or other administrator. All types of obstacles are being overcome by creative and inventive leaders of programs.

CONCLUSION

Individualized instruction offers many promises — promises of some students reaching higher levels of proficiency than was ever previously possible, and in less time — promises of happier, better satisfied students, internally motivated, who consequently stay with foreign-language study longer and may in the process learn more subject matter—promises of teachers feeling more professional and effective in their contacts with students.

It is indicated that there is something almost inherently good about individualized instruction that seems to transcend the usual considerations of what is a good instructional program. Quality becomes more important than quantity. The reduction of classroom stress reported by nearly all of the programs seems a worthwhile goal. Obviously, the fact that students are learning to educate themselves as they are being educated should be a lifetime value in our society of ever increasing knowledge. Under individualized instruction, the student is free to develop his own learning techniques, which he probably always did anyway to a certain extent, but now he has the confirmation that this is a right way.

All students have a much better opportunity to learn while engaged in individualized instruction. Students who would not be able to keep up in a classroom situation will not suffer ego damage. Students with ability and industry can accomplish unusual proficiency.

During the survey of high schools, many teachers and administrators indicated they were having some problems, but it is encouraging that every person said that they could not and would not go back to conventional classroom instruction because the students gain so much under conditions of individualized instruction.

A Bibliography of Individualized Instructional Programs Described in the Literature

Adams, Charles L. "Independence for Study." *Hispania*, L, 3 (September 1967), 483–87.

Bockman, John F. *Evaluation of a Project: Independent Foreign Language Study by Selected Eighth Graders at Townsend Junior High School Using Programmed Materials, March 3 to May 23, 1969.* Tucson, Arizona: Tucson Public Schools, 1969.

Congreve, W. J. "Independent Learning." *North Central Association Quarterly*, XL, (1965), 222–28.

Estarellas, Juan. "The Self-Instructional Foreign Language Program at Florida Atlantic University." *Hispania*, LIII, 3 (September 1970), 371–85.

Everett, Aaron B. *Syllabus for French I, II, III, New Program.* Green Springs, Ohio: Antioch College, 1967, 1968.

Fearing, Percy. "Non-graded Foreign Language Classes." *Foreign Language Annals*, II, 3, (March 1969), 343–47.

Fleury, Dale F. "Independent Study: Foreign Language Seminars." *National Association of Secondary School Principals Bulletin*, CCCXXXVIII, 53, (1969), 90–99.

Glatthorn, Allan A., et al. *An Interim Report on a Continous Progress Program in French I and Spanish I.* Abington, Pa.: Abington High School North Campus, May 1967.

Hernick, Michael, and Kennedy, Dora. "Multi-Level Grouping of Students in the Modern Foreign Language Program." *Foreign Language Annals*, II, 2, (December 1968), 200–04.

Hively, Louise F. *A Report on the Use of Color Coded Cards to Promote Individualized Instruction in Spanish Classes.* Abington, Pa.: Abington High School North Campus, June 1967.

Logan, Gerald E. "A Totally Individualized High School Program." *Individualization of Foreign Language Learning in America.* West Chester, Pennsylvania: West Chester State College, December 1970.

———. "Curricula for Individualized Instruction." *Britannica Review of Foreign Language Education, Vol. II.* Chicago: Encyclopaedia Britannica, 1970.

Masciantonio, Rudolph. "Innovative Classical Programs in the School District of Philadelphia." *Foreign Language Annals*, III, 4, (May 1970), 592–95.

Rallo, John A. "A Cooperative French Program: A New Approach." *Foreign Language Annals*, II, 4, (May 1969), 474–80.

Ruplin, Ferdinand A. and Russell, John R. "Towards Structured Foreign Language Study: An Integrated German Course." *The Modern Language Journal*, LIV, 3, (March 1970), 174–83.

Sweet, Waldo E. "Integrating Other Media with Programmed Instruction." *The Modern Language Journal*, LII, 7, (November 1968), 420–23.

Valdman, Albert. "Toward Self-Instruction in Foreign Language Learning." *International Review of American Linguistics*, II, (1964), 1–36.

———. *Advances in the Teaching of Modern Languages, II.* Edited by Gustave Mathieu. New York: Pergamon Press, 1966, 76–107.

REFERENCES

Adams, Charles L. "Independence for Study." *Hispania*, L, 3 (September 1967), 483–87.

Adams, E. N.; Morrison, H. W.; Reddy, J. M. "Conversation with a Computer as a Technique of Language Instruction." *The Modern Language Journal*, LII, 1 (January 1968), 3–16.

Altman, Howard B. "Toward a Definition of Individualized Foreign Language Instruction." *American Foreign Language Teacher*, III (February 1971).

Bloom, Benjamin S. "Learning for Mastery." *UCLA Evaluation Comment*, I, 2 (Los Angeles, 1968), 17–19.

Boyd-Bowman, Peter. "Self-Instruction in the 'Neglected' Languages: A Progress Report from Kalamazoo College." *The Modern Language Journal*, L, 1, 21–23.

Carroll, John B. "Individual Differences in Foreign Language Learning." *Proceedings: Thirty-Second Annual Foreign Language Conference at New York University*. Edited by Marvin Wasserman. New York: New York University School of Education, Division of Foreign Language and International Relations Education, 1966, 3–11.

———. "Memorandum: On Needed Research in the Psycholinguistic and Applied Psycholinguistic Aspects of Language Teaching." *Foreign Language Annals*, I, 3 (March 1968), 236–38.

Clark, William H. and Clark, Margaret G. "Achievement in Elementary German under Programmed and Conventional Instruction: A Preliminary Study." *The Modern Language Journal*, L, 2 (February 1966), 97–100.

Fearing, Percy. "Non-graded Foreign Language Classes." *Foreign Language Annals*, II, 3 (March 1969), 343–47.

Fiks, A. I. *Foreign Language Programmed Materials: 1969*. New York: MLA Materials Center, 1969.

Kersten, Caesar S. and Ott, Vesperella, E. "How Relevant Is Your Foreign Language Program?" *The Modern Language Journal*, LIV, 1 (January 1970), 9–13.

Logan, Gerald E. "Curricula for Individualized Instruction." *Britannica Review of Foreign Language Education, Vol. II*. Chicago: Encyclopaedia Britannica, 1970.

———. "A Totally Individualized High School Program." *Individualization of Foreign Language Learning in America*. West Chester, Pennsylvania: West Chester State College, December 1970, 8–10.

Mercer, David Frederick. "A Comparison of Standard Classroom and Correspondence Study Instruction in First Year High School Spanish." Doctoral Dissertation, University of Wisconsin, 1971.

Mueller, Theodore. "Programmed Instruction: Help for the Linguistically 'Underprivileged'." *The Modern Language Journal,* LII, 2 (February 1968), 79–84.

Nelson, Robert J. and Jakobovits, Leon A., Eds. "Motivation in Foreign Language Learning." *Northeast Conference on the Teaching of Foreign Languages, 1970.*

Olmo, Guillermo del. "Individualized Instruction: The Classroom Situation." *Language Learning: The Individual and the Process.* Edward W. Najam and Carleton T. Hodge, eds. *International Journal of American Linguistics,* XXXII, 1 part II (1966), 161–69.

Parent, P. Paul. "Minimizing Dropouts in the Foreign Language Program." *The Modern Language Journal,* LII, 4 (April 1968), 189–91.

Pimsleur, Paul; Sundland, Donald M.; and McIntyre, Ruth D. *Under-Achievement in Foreign Language Learning.* New York: The Modern Language Association of America, 1966.

Porter, Douglas. "A Report on Instructional Devices in Foreign Language Teaching." *Teaching Machines and Programmed Learning: A Source Book.* Edited by Arthur A. Lumsdaine and Robert Glaser. National Education Association, 1960, 186–205.

Reinert, Harry. "Student Attitudes Toward Foreign Language – No Sale!" *The Modern Language Journal,* LIV, 2 (February 1970), 107–12.

Remer, Ilo. *A Handbook for Guiding Students in Modern Foreign Languages.* Washington, D.C.: U.S. Printing Office, 1963.

Rivers, Wilga. *The Psychologist and the Foreign Language Teacher.* Chicago: The University of Chicago Press, 1964.

Steiner, Florence. "Performance Objectives in the Teaching of Foreign Languages." *Foreign Language Annals,* III, 4 (May 1970), 579–91.

Strasheim, Lorraine A. "Where From Here?" *The Modern Language Journal,* LII, 7 (November 1969), 493–97.

Sweet, Waldo E. "Integrating Other Media with Programmed Instruction." *The Modern Language Journal,* LII, 7 (November 1968), 420–23.

Valdman, Albert. "Toward Self-Instruction in Foreign Language Learning." *International Review of American Linguistics,* II (1964), 1–36.

————. *Advances in the Teaching of Modern Languages, II.* Edited by Gustave Mathieu. New York: Pergamon Press, 1966, 76–107.

Valette, Rebecca. "Teaching to Specific Objectives and Using Tests to Determine What Students Have Actually Mastered." An address delivered at the Oregon State Foreign Language Conference, October 9–10, 1970.

Zeldner, Max. "The Foreign Language Dropouts." *The Modern Language Journal,* L, 5 (May 1966), 275–80.

IX. Development of Mini-Courses at Marshall-University High School: Individualization and Interest

Mr. Donald C. Ryberg is an experienced teacher of foreign languages at the secondary and college levels. He is currently Vice President of AATSEEL, is on the staff at the University of Minnesota, and is a doctoral candidate at the university. Mr. Ryberg has developed the individualized foreign-language program at Marshall-University High School in Minneapolis.

Miss Marcia Hallock is currently on the foreign-language staff at Marshall-University High School and is a graduate student in foreign-language education at the University of Minnesota.

INTRODUCTION

Mr. Ryberg and Miss Hallock describe the development of a relevant, individualized foreign-language program and the problems of implementing individualized instruction. The discussion of mini-courses should prove especially helpful to the foreign-language teacher.

In the spring of 1968, teachers from Minneapolis' Marshall High School and University High School, the laboratory high school of the University of Minnesota, met to discuss the merger of the two schools which was to take place the following September. Although only two city blocks separated the schools, there had been little contact over the years. The schools had fulfilled very different roles. Students, staff, and community were understandably apprehensive.

However, both schools had run into difficult times. The public high school, Marshall High, was losing its population base to urban renewal, freeway building, economic decline, and an expanding university campus. An earlier study suggested closing the school and dividing its students among other schools. The University of Minnesota was finding it increasingly difficult to justify the cost of a laboratory school which was too small for wide-ranging curriculum development, too selective for generalizing research results, and too removed from what was viewed as "real life" for training teachers.

Out of these circumstances, Marshall-University High School was formed as a joint venture of the City of Minneapolis and the University of Minnesota. It was envisioned by the University as a viable laboratory school capable of performing various professional educational functions. It was seen by the public schools as a means of saving a neighborhood school and of providing a testing ground within the school system for curricular innovations. Thus, Marshall-University High School was seen not only as a marriage of convenience but as an inner-city experimental school providing opportunities for growth and change.

When the foreign-language teachers of the two merging schools met that spring to form a new Foreign Language Department for Marshall-University High School, it was inevitable that flexibility in the foreign-language program should emerge as their chief concern. The time and circumstances appeared to be ripe for rethinking goals and for establishing new priorities, yet the immediate necessity of providing on-going instruction loomed large. One of the first decisions made was that a two-year introductory language experience would be part of each student's program. Clearly, the prescribed sequencing of the typical college-oriented language program was out of place.

Thus it was that individualization of foreign-language instruction evolved as a concomitant feature of the merger. What it meant was that every effort would be made to adjust and adapt the objectives, activities, and materials of learning to the perceived needs, special interests, and specific capabilities of individual learners. So defined, individualization of instruction was acceptable to everyone because it allowed a maximum amount of flexibility and because it focused on learning and the learner.

Of course, no curriculum is completely innovative. Underlying factors and conditions inevitably dictate outcomes. The parameters which shaped the foreign-language program at Marshall-University High School were (1) size of school; (2) diversity of students; (3) physical plant; (4) funding; (5) scheduling.

(1) *Size of school.* Marshall-University High School is a relatively small school. Since there are only 1250 students spread across grades 7–12, options offered them are necessarily limited.

(2) *Diversity of students.* Roughly seventy-five percent of the students who attend Marshall-University High School do so because they live in the district. As former students of Marshall High School, they were used to the traditional, relatively conservative public-school education that they were offered. Their families range from professional people including many university professors to working-class people to low-income residents of a federally-funded housing project in the district.

The remaining students can be divided into three categories. First, there are the former students of University High School, a generally sophisticated, highly-motivated, liberally-oriented group from middle- and upper-middle-class families throughout the Metropolitan area. Secondly, there are the orthopedically and hearing handicapped students who come from all over the city; and finally, there is a group of students, also from all over the city, who are participating in Minneapolis' voluntary transfer program to achieve racial balance in the schools. This third group is a highly vocal and generally liberal minority. Reconciling their demands for relevance and educational alternatives with traditional conservatism was a paramount consideration from the first.

(3) *Physical plant.* As was mentioned earlier, the merger brought together two buildings located two blocks apart. The main building, formerly Marshall High School, is nearly fifty years old. Its classrooms are solid and inflexible, isolated from one another in long rows along dark and depressing corridors. The foreign-language classrooms are clustered together in this building.

The other building, formerly University High School, is relatively new and well-designed. However, the University of Minnesota departmental offices and classes that it also houses make it a somewhat alien atmosphere for students in a central city school.

(4) *Funding.* Unfortunately, as is so often the case, the really essential ingredients for innovation were missing. There was neither the time for planning and developing objectives nor the money for creating the new and different materials that the proposed program of individualized instruction demanded. It is to the credit of the Foreign Language Staff that Marshall-University High School's program succeeded as well as it did in its first

years, since what money was available was earmarked for commercial materials and equipment.

(5) *Scheduling*. The final and perhaps crucial problem, still unresolved, was the constraint imposed by arbitrary divisions of time. Student schedules, length of periods, academic units of time, and time as a function of attaining objectives all interact with teaching objectives, teacher assignments, sequencing and articulation from level to level as well as with the utilization of materials, equipment, and facilities to best advantage. Flexibility in a foreign-language program is much more difficult to achieve within rigid allotments of time.

Since Marshall-University's doors opened in September, 1968, its foreign-language teachers have been working with a wide range of structures for implementing individualized instruction. These structures range all the way from the lock-step classroom featuring student-centered enrichment activities to completely individualized programs written for specific students. Some of the most successful implementing structures for individualization that have been used are Independent Study and Directed Readings programs. Others include such variant structures as Self-Pacing, Continuous Progress, Mastery Learning, Ability Grouping, and the use of Multiple Materials. The former structures seem particularly well suited to advanced students and the latter to beginning and intermediate students where they can be used within even the most traditional and rigid scheduling patterns.

Because the latter implementing structures are most useful at the early levels of language instruction and can be used in self-contained classrooms, the foreign-language department decided during the first year that revitalizing intermediate- and advanced-level programs should have top priority. Further, high-school students at that time were just beginning to demand increased relevance in subject matter as well as increased input into educational policy and decision-making. Realizing that the creation of individual programs on demand for all intermediate and advanced students would be an impossible task, the staff began to cast about for an implementing structure which would provide flexibility, student input, relevance to student interests and goals, independent study and interest grouping.

Many ideas were discussed and considered. The Unipac or individual learning package concept was gaining popularity, but very few were yet available in the foreign languages and the topics covered tended to be rather traditional. Further, structures such as Independent Study, Directed Readings, and Learning Packages were intended mainly for students working alone. It was felt that communication and the motivation provided through the dynamics of a closely-knit class might be passed over or neglected if these structures were used exclusively.

At this point, several of the teachers began to discuss possibilities with students, both casually outside the classroom and in classroom discussions. It became increasingly clear that few students were satisfied with the language-learning materials being used. They were especially disparaging of the multi-level texts used in long sequences in which students are expected to engage in the same kinds of learning activities year after year, modified only minimally from level to level. No matter how carefully prepared and sequenced these materials may be, no matter how culturally authentic, many students clearly feel they are "stifling pedagogic devices" and not the "real stuff" of living language.

Further, students were decidedly outspoken about the passive role they must play in teacher-oriented classrooms. They were raised in front of the television screen where they passively watched the world drift by. There seems to be little new or exotic left for them. Marshall-University language teachers acknowledged quite frankly that they were unable to compete hour after hour with even standard television productions costing thousands of dollars to produce.

The implications were clear. Students want to use authentic language resources as soon as possible. They want to be actively involved in the process of learning, i.e., actively participating while studying relevant content in the foreign language. What struck the Marshall-University High School foreign language teachers was that student preferences and traditional foreign language teaching objectives are in no sense opposed: learners should be actively involved in the learning process and the final result should be language proficiency, i.e., the capability for using language as a tool for communication and information gathering. Yet, it seems that over the years teaching methods have estranged the two. This realization gave birth to the guiding principle that curriculum reorganization must be based on relevant, student-chosen subject content with active and creative student participation—not mindless mimicking or meaningless manipulation of contrived language patterns.

The first step to discover relevant student-centered subject content was taken by Shirley Krogmeier, Paul Schweppe, and Margaret Shryer, Marshall-University German teachers. They began to discuss some of the possibilities for change with their intermediate and advanced classes. Next, they asked students to list the areas of study related to German language and culture which interested them the most. The students listed nearly sixty possibilities which ranged all the way from such predictable ones as German Popular Music and German Cooking to such surprising choices as Advanced Grammar.

At this point the teachers analyzed the list carefully. They combined topics that appeared to be similar, modified others somewhat to make them more suitable to available materials, and grouped them under the categories of Language Skills and Special Interests. In addition, they added several topics which they felt would be especially interesting and appropriate, but which might have been beyond the students' realm of knowledge. From this master list, students were asked to choose those topics which appealed to them most and to rank them in order from one to five. This ranking of topics in German became the basis for the mini-course or elective-within-an-elective program at Marshall-University High School.

It was a short step to formalizing the program — with the cautious realization, of course, that formalization could bring its own kind of rigidity. With the enthusiastic encouragement of Marshall-University's Director, Dr. Almon G. Hoye, and the public school's Foreign-Language Constultant, Dr. Jermaine D. Arendt, other language teachers surveyed their students in various ways in order to arrive at similar subject topics.

A sampling of the course titles which were finally selected follows:

French
   Un Voyage En France
   France Today: A Comparison
   Skills Workshop
   The French Canadian
   Advanced Grammar
   Written Expression
German
   Deutschlandreise
   Grammar Review
   Journalism

Scientific German Through Films
News Media
Correspondence: Business and Personal
Russian
  The Soviets and Their Land
  Advanced Grammar
  USSR: Current Topics
  Technical Readings
  Vocabulary Building
  Soviet Readings
Spanish
  Travel Through Mexico and Central America
  Political Independence and Power in Latin America
  Reading the Masters
  Patterns of Spanish
  Test Taking
  Commercial Spanish

Once subject topics were determined, individual teachers began setting up courses. Since mini-courses are meant to be prepared "on demand" for specific groups of students with special interests in common, it is expected that they will vary greatly from year to year. Therefore, little attempt has been made to formalize them, except for purposes of departmental record keeping.

Barbara Gunderson, a French teacher, has developed a guide which provides a format for course development. This flexible guide lists the essential components of a mini-course:

  I. *Course title*
  II. *Course description*
      A. General description
      B. Prerequisites
      C. Scheduling
      D. Credit
  III. *Objectives*
  IV. *Content*
  V. *Learning strategy*
      A. Pre-test
      B. Conditions of learning
      C. Learning activities
      D. Functions of components
  VI. *Learning components*
      A. Commerical materials

    B. Teacher-prepared materials

    C. Community resources

    D. Equipment

    E. Realia

VII. *Resources*

    A. Bibliography

    B. Films

    C. Records

    D. Tapes

    E. Etc.

The course description provided for in the guide appears in the students' registration handbook. Several examples follow:

FRENCH SKILLS WORKSHOP

One credit, offered 1st quarter only

Prerequisites: Second-year French or Departmental Permission

This course is a "potpourri" (mixture) of activities aimed at up-grading the listening, speaking, reading and writing skills of the student through practice and participation. It is for the student who does not wish to concentrate on any particular skill, but who wants to improve his pronunciation, pick up hints on how to read French better, build up his vocabulary, work on constructing sentences, spell correctly, and improve his understanding of spoken French.

GERMAN CORRESPONDENCE: BUSINESS AND PERSONAL

One credit, offered 3rd quarter only

Prerequisites: Second-year German or Departmental Permission

Students are initiated into the art of letter writing as a means of communication. In addition to the formal study of the parts of the personal and business letter, the student practices his writing in actual correspondence (e.g., writing to pen pals in German-speaking countries or to other students of German in the United States). Business letters include ordering items from mail order catalogues in Germany, applying for summer jobs in German-speaking countries, and requesting information about vacation accommodations.

THE SOVIETS AND THEIR LAND

One credit, offered 1st quarter only

Prerequisites: Third-year Russian or Departmental Permission

The Soviet individual and his relationship to his world will be studied. Changes in his way of life as a result of revolution, world war, economics and expansionism will be considered. Contrasts with American culture and society will be stressed.

SPANISH TEST TAKING

One credit, offered 3rd quarter only
Prerequisites: Second-year Spanish or Departmental Permission

Students study from a large variety of available tests. They investigate ways to improve test scores, particularly in preparing for College Board Exams and placement tests. This course serves as a grammar review and stresses vocabulary development.

Since tentative planning for the following school year was geared to an open and flexible schedule, the language department, in consultation with the Director, decided on a model which would allow students to combine one, two, or three mini-courses in parallel. This would mean studying each content area selected for perhaps two or three hours weekly including both class time and independent directed study. Spring pre-registration for Fall classes indicated that the students were enthusiastic. Students were able to register for partial credit programs in cases where specialty requirements might have forced them to drop foreign-language classes in other years or other schools. Others pre-registered for more than single credits.

After pre-registration tallies were in, a chain of circumstances occurred in late spring and summer which led to the retention of the standard six-period school day. This meant that foreign-language students were not only *not* scheduled according to their expressed choices, but that all intermediate and advanced students were scheduled into *mixed* classes *regardless* of grade level or language proficiency.

Thus, during 1970–71, students *had* to compromise. However, to the extent that it was possible during the class hours in which they were scheduled, they selected the mini-courses on a considerably limited basis. Classes were then grouped according to these interests, and students attended class either for parts of scheduled periods or only on certain days of the week. The remainder of their time was spent in independent, directed study. Many of the students used the facilities of the Foreign Language Resource Center regularly for their independent study.

During the course of the year, the faculty and administration of the school planned a major change in the division of the school year. It was decided to change from two 18-week *Semesters* to three 12-week *Trimesters*. This change would provide for the future development of a *fourth* 12-week *Quarter* during the summer months. In accord with this decision, mini-courses were reorganized and students were again pre-registered. In the meantime, however, the school district was awarded a large federal grant, with the result that immediate changes are being delayed pending more general reorganization of school programs and structure.

Meanwhile, mini-courses will be operated on a "demand" basis for another year. Students will select their preferences at the beginning of each academic Quarter. Classes and study time will then be arranged individually, depending upon each student's particular schedule. Thus, in modifying the mini-course program, a great deal of flexibility has been discovered even within a traditional school schedule and system of student programming.

On the other hand, it is not surprising that students and teachers alike were discouraged when their expectations could not be fully realized. Some attrition inevitably occurred. However, after only three years, approximately 55% of the student body is enrolled in foreign languages. This figure is considerably higher than the percentage enrolled in foreign languages at old Marshall High School and, in three years, the first cycle of students will complete grades 7 through 12.

The mini-course concept will probably continue to be the basic organizing structure for individualizing the senior high-school foreign-language program. Students appear to like it and regularly bring in fresh ideas for new topics. In addition to allowing them input into curricular decisions, it gives them a much wider variety of learning experiences and introduces them to the foreign culture from numerous aspects. Further, no single course is of such duration that it becomes boring or intolerable. Finally, teachers are particularly careful to apply objectives and evaluation criteria flexibly, in order to account equitably for individual differences.

The flexibility of the mini-course allows concomitant options as well. Some students continue to pursue independent study projects or programs of directed readings. Typically, these options are proposed by students themselves under a study contract. Objectives are outlined in advance and acceptable procedures must be proposed for evaluation. The degree of supervision required depends largely on the individual's past record of performance. Teacher-student conferences vary from semi-weekly to infrequent meetings.

Increasingly, students are receiving foreign-language credit for study completed *outside* of the Foreign Language Department. Several students have received credits both in Literature courses or Social Studies and in Foreign Languages when the reading has been done in the language they are studying. Foreign study and travel credits have been equated and granted as well. Plans are currently underway for a study of ecological problems in other countries—an inter-disciplinary possibility including Social Studies, Science, and Foreign Languages. An inter-disciplinary mini-course in Comparative Linguistics will be offered in 1971–72. Credit may be earned *either* in Foreign Languages *or* in English.

In addition, a number of students have enrolled, by special arrangement, in foreign-language courses at the University of Minnesota. Several students have enrolled in less-commonly taught languages: Hebrew, Italian, Swedish, and Japanese. Others have enrolled in advanced sections of languages studied at Marshall-University High. These students may elect to receive high school and/or university credits, although regular university tuition is required if the latter option is elected.

During the summer of 1971, Shirley Krogmeier, Barbara Gunderson, Marcia Hallock, and Donald Ryberg worked with innovative intensive foreign-language programs. Miss Gunderson also conducted a small intensive French course as a pilot program during the school year 1970–71. Such programs present exciting possibilities for schools with open and flexible schedules. Plans have been made already to implement certain aspects of these programs, especially activity-oriented projects and expanded use of community resources. It is hoped that increased flexibility within Marshall-University High School will someday permit intensive language experiences for all students.

Flexibility and individualization have become key words for Foreign Language Teachers at Marshall-University High School. Particular implementing structures such as mini-courses may not suit every school. However, the practical emphasis on flexibility as opposed to rigidity, is valid everywhere as is the focus on learning rather than teaching. The key words, of course, imply that curricular development is a dynamic, never-ending process.

X. Foreign Languages in John Dewey High School, New York City: An Individualized Approach

Mr. Stephen Levy is an experienced secondary-school teacher of foreign languages. He is currently Chairman of the Department of Foreign Languages at John Dewey High School in New York City. Mr. Levy presented his program recently at the Northeast Conference for Teachers of Foreign Languages in New York (1971).

INTRODUCTION

Mr. Levy discusses John Dewey High School, a secondary school using modular scheduling, encouraging individualized instruction in all academic areas. His thorough exploration of all phases of the foreign-language program should provide helpful information for the foreign-language teacher or teacher trainer.

John Dewey High School is the first experimental non-graded high school in the New York City Public School System. It opened in September, 1969, with an initial enrollment of one thousand students. During the next two years, it added another thousand students to the enrollment each year, bringing the present enrollment to its maximum of three thousand students.

Prior to the discussion of the individualization of instruction in foreign languages at John Dewey High School, it is necessary to explain the essential nature of the over-all school program, because there are many features in the basic organization of the school that make the concept and practice of individualized instruction a viable and, in fact, an inherent part of its philosophy.

The plans for this high school were formulated by a group of high-school principals who were commissioned to design a high school that would provide young people with an education to meet the challenges of modern life. Their plan was published by the Board of Education of the City of New York and is entitled "The New High School — A School For Our Times." The school that these administrators proposed is radically different, yet realistic and practicable. It is based on the principle that every student should be required to achieve a reasonable mastery of an area of knowledge before he may advance. This new school encourages acceleration and enrichment, reduces the penalty of failure, and stimulates effort. Each student may advance at his own rate, thereby affording some students the opportunity to be graduated in two years, others in three, and others in a longer period of time. The responsibility for learning is thrown on the student, where it belongs.

Some of the features of the plan for this high school include the abolition of grade levels, the discontinuation of the Carnegie Unit as a measure of progress, the abolition of the five-period-per-week lockstep through modular and flexible scheduling, the abandonment of the distinction between major and minor subjects, the provision for instruction in practical arts for college-bound as well as work-oriented students, the incorporation of extra-class activities into the curriculum, the involvement of the classroom teacher in guidance, the utilization of new methods and modern technology to supplement conventional instructional procedures, and the implementation of a longer school day. The new school is intended for students of *all* levels of ability, not for a special group.

The original plan incorporated the concept of five phases of seven-week duration, non-gradedness both in grouping and in reporting the achievement of the students, an intramural sports program, typing for all students, extra curricular activities built into an extended school day and the concept of the resource center.

Over the past two years, this original plan has been implemented into an actual working format of the following nature: the school year is divided into 5 seven-week cycles, each approximately thirty-five days in duration. Every seven weeks, students and teachers receive new programs. An optional summer session provides a sixth cycle, and thus the school is in operation almost all year. The students and teachers have an eight-hour day that is divided into twenty-two modules of twenty-minute duration.

The basic configuration of the schedule came about through common agreement between the chairmen and the principal for a type of program that offers the most effective instruction in terms of distribution of time. Chart 1 indicates the master con-

CHART 1: MASTER CONFIGURATION OF THE MODULAR SCHEDULE
(JOHN DEWEY HIGH SCHOOL, NEW YORK CITY)

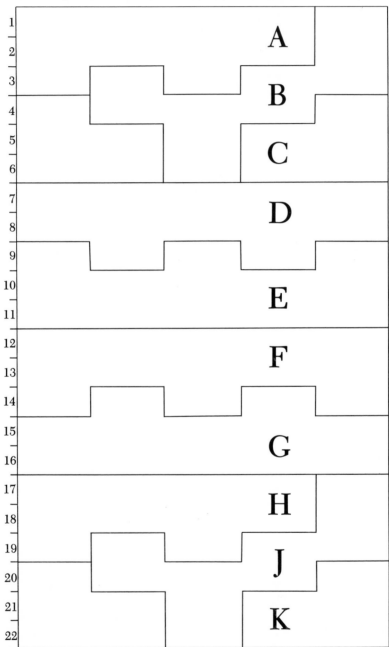

figuration on which all department programs are built. Classes can be scheduled for two consecutive modules across the board (Configurations D, E, F, G); for three one-hour classes per week (Configurations E, F); or for a combination of two consecutive modules twice a week and three consecutive modules twice a week (Configurations A, B, C, D, E, F, G, H, J, K). What this configuration also does is to limit the number of students who have independent study or self-directed time at the same time, thereby maximizing the use of the physical plant and the teacher resources. It also provides for a more regular pattern of independent study for students, enabling them to establish a set meeting time with a teacher in the resource center.

Chart 2 is a copy of a student's program. It reflects the total school program in terms of the subjects that the student is taking, the meeting time of the classes fitted into the basic configuration as presented in Chart 1, and the concept of independent study or self-directed time.

Chart 3 is a copy of a teacher's program. Every teacher teaches five classes and in addition serves twenty-five modules per week in the resource center. Building assignments are rotated among the teachers every seven weeks.

The eight-hour day gives the students time for "Independent Study." These times are modules on the pupil's program when he is free to choose how he will spend his time. The amount of independent study time varies from student to student, depending on how many subjects he is taking. The decision as to where and how the student will spend his "Independent Study" time is left to the student. However, each subject area has its own resource center which is a satellite library, an audio-visual center, and a place to get tutorial help, to do homework or to work on an advanced individual project.

The two basic cornerstones of John Dewey High School are individual progress and independent study. Individual progress is achieved by the seven-week organization. At the end of each seven weeks, the student's work is evaluated for that period of time. The grading system is neither numerical nor letter equivalent. The students are given a rating of "Mastery" (M), "Mastery With Condition" (MC), or "Retention For Reinforcement" (R). The student who is rated "M" moves ahead into the next phase of work. The "MC" student also moves ahead, but the teacher writes a prescription for him in which he lists the student's weaknesses and makes suggestions for removing these deficiences. The "R" student also receives a prescription form,

CHART 2: SAMPLE OF A PUPIL'S PROGRAM. (JOHN DEWEY HIGH SCHOOL, NEW YORK CITY)

Name _____ ID: _____ Offcl _____

Mod	Monday	Room	Tuesday	Room	Wednesday	Room	Thursday	Room	Friday	Room
1	Frenchc4 3	245	Frenchc4 3	245	Frenchc4 3	245	Frenchc4 3	245	Cons Eco 2	357
2	Frenchc4 3	245	Frenchc4 3	245	Frenchc4 3	245	Frenchc4 3	245	Cons Eco 2	357
3	Frenchc4 3	245	Cons Eco 2	357	Frenchc4 3	245	Cons Eco 2	357	Cons Eco 2	357
4	Theater 1	221	Cons Eco 2	357	Cons Eco 2	357	Cons Eco 2	357	Theater 1	221
5	Theater 1	221	Theater 1	221	Cons Eco 2	357	Theater 1	221	Theater 1	221
6	Theater 1	221	Theater 1	221	Cons Eco 2	357	Theater 1	221	Theater 1	221
7	Ind Study		Biology544	344	Biology544	344	Biology544	344	Biology544	344
8	Ind Study		Biology544	344	Biology544	344	Biology544	344	Biology544	344
9	Ind Study		Biology544	344	Biology544	344	Biology544	344	Chambmus 8	A5
10	Ind Study		Chambmus 8	A5	Chambmus 8	A5	Chambmus 8	A5	Chambmus 8	A5
11	Ind Study		Chambmus 8	A5	Chambmus 8	A5	Chambmus 8	A5	Chambmus 8	A5
12	Lunch		Lunch		Lunch		Lunch		Lunch	
13	Lunch		Lunch		Lunch		Lunch		Lunch	
14	Lunch		Gamepuzzl5	349	Lunch		Gamepuzzl5	349	Lunch	
15	Gamepuzzl5	349	Gamepuzzl5	349	Gamepuzzl5	349	Gamepuzzl5	349	Ind Study	349
16	Gamepuzzl5	349	Gamepuzzl5	349	Gamepuzzl5	349	Gamepuzzl5	349	Ind Study	349
17	Geom 74 5	302	Geom 74 5	302	Geom 74 5	302	Geom 74 5	302	Sten 01 6	380
18	Geom 74 5	302	Geom 74 5	302	Geom 74 5	302	Geom 74 5	302	Sten 01 6	380
19	Geom 74 5	302	Sten 01 6	380	Geom 74 5	302	Sten 01 6	380	Sten 01 6	380
20	Physedg 9	G15	Sten 01 6	380	Sten 01 6	380	Sten 01 6	380	Physedg 9	G15
21	Physedg 9	G15	Physedg 9	G15	Sten 01 6	380	Physedg 9	G15	Physedg 9	G15
22	Physedg 9	G15	Physedg 9	G15	Sten 01 6	380	Physedg 9	G15	Physedg 9	G15

CHART 3: SAMPLE OF A TEACHER'S PROGRAM (JOHN DEWEY HIGH SCHOOL, NEW YORK CITY). Legend: 376/01 — Spanish, Level II, Phase 4; 371/01 — Spanish, Level I, Phase 4; 369/02 — Spanish, Level I, Phase 3; (The number following the slash indicates the class section); R.C. — Resource Center.

JOHN DEWEY HIGH SCHOOL FOREIGN LANGUAGE DEPARTMENT
Sol Levine, Principal Stephen L. Levy, Chairman
Teacher's Program Notification Form
Dear *Mrs. Cenac:*
This is a copy of your program for cycle 4, beginning on March 8, 1971.

Mod.	Monday Class	Room	Tuesday Class	Room	Wednesday Class	Room	Thursday Class	Room	Friday Class	Room
1	376/01	267	376/01	267	376/01	267	376/01	267	371/01	265
2	376/01	267	376/01	267	376/01	267	376/01	267	371/01	265
3	376/01	267	371/01	265	376/01	267	371/01	265	371/01	265
4	R.C.	261	371/01	265	371/01	265	371/01	265	R.C.	261
5	R.C.	261	R.C.	261	371/01	265	R.C.	261	R.C.	261
6	R.C.	261	R.C.	261	371/01	265	R.C.	261	R.C.	261
7										
8										
9	376/03	267			R.C.	261			376/03	267
10	376/03	267	376/03	267	R.C.	261	376/03	267	376/03	267
11	376/03	267	376/03	267	R.C.	261	376/03	267	376/03	267
12	L	U	N		C		H			
13										
14			369/02	267	R.C.	261	369/02	267	R.C.	261
15	369/02	267	369/02	267	369/02	267	369/02	267	Prep.	
16	369/02	267	369/02	267	369/02	267	369/02	267		
17									371/06	265
18		Preparation							371/06	265
19			371/06	265			371/06	265	371/06	265
20	R.C.	261	371/06	265	371/06	265	371/06	265	R.C.	261
21	R.C.	261	R.C.	261	371/06	265	R.C.	261	R.C.	261
22	R.C.	261	R.C.	261	371/06	265	R.C.	261	R.C.	261

but he is not moved ahead. Since he has not mastered the objectives of this phase of work, he is not subjected to the more complex tasks of the next more advanced phase. Instead, the prescription form serves as the basis of the work the student does during the next seven weeks. Retention is only for seven weeks rather than for six months or a year as is done in other New York City high schools. A sample of the prescription form that is used in the foreign-language department is presented in Chart 4. It is correlated with our "Supportive DISK" which we created to help the "MC" student succeed in the next phase of work in foreign languages.

The "Supportive DISK" is a device by which the student who has received "MC" in the previous phase of a course is directed in mastering the objectives of that phase of work in which he manifested weakness. The "Supportive DISK" is an overview of the topics and objectives that were covered during the phase. On this overview are listed the topics and the objectives and specific exercises and tapes that the student should use to help him master these objectives. The student is given a specified amount of time, which is negotiable with his new subject class teacher, in which to complete the topics listed on his prescription form. This work is done in the resource center where the student has the facility of getting one-to-one help from the teachers who serve there.

Thus, individual progress is achieved by dividing the school year into five seven-week cycles. At the end of each cycle, the student is rated by the teacher and based on his mastery of the objectives of the course, he is either moved ahead into the next phase of the course or he is retained for reinforcement. These reorganizations, in addition to effecting the proper placement of students in courses most suited to their needs, also have a most favorable effect on the school atmosphere and school morale as there is, in essence, a rebirth every seven weeks. The students feel that they are beginning fresh again, most often with a different teacher, and this adds enthusiasm to their outlook. (The summer session, which keeps our school open almost all year, is optional both for students and teachers.)

The other cornerstone of our school is "Independent Study." There are various levels of independent study and they can all be observed in operation at John Dewey. The student may simply choose to spend some of his independent study time in "leisure"-type activities of a recreational nature. He may also do his home-

John Dewey High School
Sol Levine, Principal

Foreign Language Department
Stephen L. Levy, Chairman

COMMENT ON
INDIVIDUAL PROGRESS

PRESCRIPTION FORM

_____
Student's Last Name

_____
First Name

_____
I.D. Number

_____
Off. Class

_____
Present Subject Section

_____
Current School Cycle

_____
Subject Teacher

☐ Mastery With Condition   ☐ Retention for Reinforcement
THIS PRESCRIPTION IS TO BE USED IN CONJUNCTION
WITH THE OVERVIEW SHEET GIVEN TO YOU BY YOUR
SUBJECT CLASS TEACHER THIS PHASE.

Comments:
☐ Excessive Absence: _____ times this cycle.
☐ Improvement needed in study habits, particularly in the
preparation of homework assignments.
☐ Improvement needed in being prepared each day in class
with the proper textbook, notebook and pen.

Structures: Overview   ☐ Completed   ☐ Incomplete
☐ (   )
  (   )
  (   )

Reading and Vocabulary: Class Participation:
☐ (   )   ☐
  (   )
  (   )

Civilization: Oral Ability/Auditory Comprehension
☐   ☐

N.B. The number given in parenthesis corresponds to the topic
on your OVERVIEW SHEET.

work during this time. By going to the appropriate resource center, he can get assistance in his assignment from the teacher who is assigned to the center or from one of the student teachers. There is also a group of advanced students in foreign languages who have volunteered to serve as tutors in the resource center during certain modules. Independent study time may also be used for remediation whereby the student, aware of a need for help with a particular objective, or advised by his teacher to work on a specific task, goes to the resource center. Independent study in its highest form is engaged in by students who choose to study a foreign language completely on their own. We offer independent study in the four languages that we offer in formal classes: French, Hebrew, Italian, and Spanish. We also offer programs in German, Russian, and Latin. These students receive a DISK (Dewey Independent Study Kit) and they work on their own or get help in the resource center. Mastery of the objectives set forth in the DISK gives the student the grade of "MI" or Mastery in Independent Study, and permits him to move on to the next phase of work.

The physical plant is conducive to the program and philosophy of John Dewey High School. Each subject area has its own resource center, and built around the center are five classrooms with movable walls to provide for large- and small-group instruction. The resource center can be used as an adjunct of the classroom because three of the classrooms have windows that open into the resource center, and the teacher can monitor the students he sends into the resource center to work on a specific task or project. Chart 5 shows the physical set-up of the foreign-language department.

The resource center is a vital and integral part of our program. An informal teaching-learning situation exists in the resource center between pupils and the teachers who serve there. It is in the resource center that we employ differentiated staffing. Each teacher works an additional hour and forty minutes daily and spends this time in the resource center working directly with the students. In addition to the licensed teacher, we have student teachers, our own advanced students who serve as tutors, and para-professionals. Ideally, the para-professionals who work in the language resource center would also have some foreign-language training so that they could help students with work there. Even if they are not so qualified, they facilitate the distribution and control of materials that are available for use in the resource center. These materials include copies of the textbooks that are

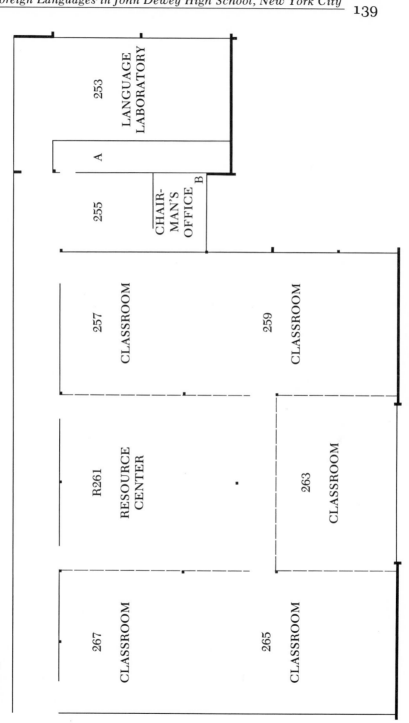

CHART 5

used in our classes, supplementary textbooks that are used as reference or resource materials, language newspapers and magazines, worksheets that have been prepared by the teachers, and our "tape of the week" program. There is also audio-visual equipment in the resource center in the form of a tape recorder, a phonograph, and filmstrip viewers. Study carrels afford students privacy when they work. A copy of the student's prescription form is also kept in the resource center so that the teacher can give the student more meaningful assistance. To be included in the resource center is a "Dial Access" program that will provide the students with more opportunities to work with tapes in foreign languages.

The Language Laboratory plays a dual role in the foreign-language department. It is used by all the classes in the department as they are programmed into the lab at least once every two weeks. The other function of the language laboratory is that of a resource center, and it is used in this capacity during the modules when no class is scheduled to be there. The students come into the laboratory, take the tape they need, and get to work. They are monitored by a teacher who is assigned there to help them.

The language laboratory has four decks and thirty-six student positions. Thirty positions are audio-active and the other six have the facility to record what the student is saying. The materials that are used in the lab are the commercial tapes that accompany our textbook series, structure tapes that have been prepared by the Bureau of Audio-Visual Instruction of the Board of Education of the City of New York, and tapes that the teachers in the department have prepared.

The learning activities are, by and large, teacher directed. When his class meets, the teacher is free to break up the time blocks into a variety of activities. The language classes meet only four times per week: twice a week for two consecutive modules and twice a week for three consecutive modules. The longer class period gives the teacher more freedom in varying the classroom situation.

As a means of individualizing instruction and capitalizing on the strengths of the teachers in the department, we have implemented team teaching. Two classes of the same level and phase are programmed for the same time slot and placed in adjoining classrooms with movable walls. The teachers of these classes plan their lessons together and bring both classes together for various activities. While one teacher works with the large group, the other teacher either circulates around the room offering individual attention to students or works with selected students from both classes in the other classroom on some objective in which these students need help.

Our most exciting endeavor in individualizing instruction in foreign languages is through the "open classroom." The rationale behind this concept is that a child should progress at his own individual rate and master a specific objective by achieving a predetermined performance criterion. We all know that no two individuals are exactly alike and therefore we cannot expect them to learn in exactly the same way. Boredom, partial student involvement and passivity are all the results of the traditional concept of teaching a lesson to an entire class, despite the superior quality and effectiveness of the teaching techniques employed. In the open classroom, the student is directly and actively involved and responsible for his own learning. It is a learning center free of the restraints of the traditional classroom, and the student works at his own self-determined pace and in the manner in which he is most comfortable. Thus he is led into accepting total responsibility for his work. Another outcome of this change of milieu is that his attitude changes and becomes more positive, and eventually he develops an enthusiasm for the subject, ingredients that are vital for true learning to take place.

Setting up an open classroom is not an easy chore. The teacher must pre-plan every step of the operation and offer close and constant supervision in the day-to-day development of the program. Where does the teacher begin? First, he prepares instruction sheets for the students in which he lists the procedures they are to follow in the open classroom. It is also important to include an instruction sheet on how to do the various types of lessons. (See Charts 6, 7, 8.) The next big job is to prepare the overview of the work that the students are to cover during the phase. In this way the students know specifically what topics they must master during the phase. Then, for each topic on the overview, the

CHART 6

John Dewey High School	Foreign Language Department
Sol Levine, Principal	Stephen L. Levy, Chairman

Learning a Foreign Language Through the Open Classroom

Here is the most important information about the new way class will be organized:

1. You will receive an overview of the topics to be mastered for this phase.

2. For each topic on the overview, there will be a packet of materials that will guide you in mastering the topic. You must complete all the work in the packet and then hand it in to your teacher.

3. Before you may proceed to the next topic, you must know whether you have mastered the previous topic. On every structure topic there will be a quiz. On every two stories there will be a quiz. YOU MUST MASTER A TOPIC BEFORE YOU GO ON TO THE NEXT ONE. You will take the test when you feel you are ready.

4. In preparing the work for each unit to achieve mastery of the topic, you may do any of the following: work alone, work with one or several friends, work with tapes, work with a teacher aide, or work with your teacher.

5. Obviously, full class lectures will be abolished. If you need explanations, you will have to ASK for them. They will be given personally or in small groups.

6. In order to provide for large group practice in auditory comprehension and auditory dialogues, we will from time to time reassemble the class for a large group activity.

7. Teacher assigned homework has been abolished, but self-assigned homework has NOT. It is still expected that you will work outside of class, at home and in the Resource Center.

CHART 7

John Dewey High School   Foreign Language Department
Sol Levine, Principal   Stephen L. Levy, Chairman
                        Reading Lesson

                        General Instructions

General Objective: To read the story with the goal of comprehension of the ideas presented in it without translation into English, and to demonstrate your mastery of these ideas by writing out various drills.

Introduction:

The story you are about to read has been divided into parts. For each segment of the story, your worksheet gives you an objective for that part of the story, a list of selected words with which you may not be familiar, and a drill based on what you have read that will help you check your achievement of the objective. DO ALL WORK IN THE FIRST SEGMENT BEFORE GOING ON TO THE SECOND.

Procedures for each segment of the story:

1. Read the objective of this part.

2. To read this part with direct comprehension, you must understand the key words. Read the list of words on the worksheet. These are important words which you may not already know. Begin to compile a personal vocabulary section listing those words that are new to you. Write the word and its meaning and then think about words related to this word, such as possible synonyms, antonyms or other words that come from this word. For example: To bake, baker, bakery; cold—(antonym) hot; happy—(synonym) cheerful.

3. Now read the segment for the first time. There may be other words in it which you don't know or recognize. Do the following with these words:

    a. Write the word in your personal vocabulary list.

    b. Look up the meaning in the vocabulary section of the book or in the dictionary.

    c. Write the meaning next to the word.

    d. Think about and list possible synonyms, antonyms or other words that come from this word.

    These steps will result in increasing your vocabulary.

4. Now reread this section to understand it without English and to be aware of what happens in it. After the second reading, do the exercise on your worksheet to check your mastery of the section.

5. Now go back to the objective of this section. ANSWER THE QUESTION OF THE OBJECTIVE IN THE FOREIGN LANGUAGE.

REPEAT THIS PROCEDURE FOR EACH PART OF THE STORY.

Summary:

Now that you have read the entire story, it's a good idea to see if you have mastered the basic objective, that is, to read the story with complete comprehension in the foreign language.

1. <u>Do the drills in your book</u> indicated on your worksheet.
2. To see how well you can put everything together, <u>select one</u> <u>of the following types of exercises</u> to show your personal comprehension of the story.

    a. Using key words indicated on the worksheet, <u>write a</u> <u>summary</u> around them.

    b. <u>Write a brief ORIGINAL summary</u> (about 5 sentences) of the story.

    c. Create a dialogue between two people in which their conversation reflects the main ideas of the story.

CHART 8

John Dewey High School   Foreign Language Department
Sol Levine, Principal   Stephen L. Levy, Chairman

Structure Lesson

General Instructions

<u>General Objective</u>: To master a specific grammatical concept which shows how words are put together in a certain way to give a desired meaning in the foreign language. For example:

In English we say: I am 15 years old.
In French we say: J'ai 15 ans.
In Italian we say: Io ho 15 anni.
In Spanish we say: Tengo 15 años.
In Hebrew we say: אני בן 15.

Introduction:

The lesson you are about to do has been divided into parts. For each part of the lesson your worksheet gives you:

1. an objective for that part of the lesson.
2. several model sentences which illustrate the objective.
3. a generalization that explains the concept of that objective.
4. suggested drills that will test your understanding and application of this objective.
5. a pattern drill to practice ORALLY with a classmate who is also working on this lesson.

DO ALL WORK IN THE FIRST PART BEFORE GOING ON TO THE SECOND.

Procedures for each part of the lesson:

1. Read the objective.

2. Read the model sentences and be sure that you understand everything contained in them.

3. Read the generalization and then go back to the model sentences to be sure you understand how it applies to each of them.

4. Do the suggested drill exercises.

5. Do the pattern drill ORALLY with a classmate.

REPEAT THIS PROCEDURE FOR EACH PART OF THE LESSON.

Summary:

Now that you have studied the entire lesson, it is a good idea to see if you have mastered the basic objective, that is, to use this structure in a natural way as you speak or write the language.

1. Do the drills in your book indicated on your worksheet.

2. To see how well you can put everything together, select one of the following types of exercises:

    a. Make up original sentences to illustrate each of the objectives in this lesson.

    b. Create a brief dialogue in which you incorporate the new structure you have mastered in this lesson.

teacher must prepare the learning packet that the students will work with. It is the written work that the students do in answering the questions and in writing out the drills that provides the student with a very clear picture of his mastery of the topic. How the student will work is left up **to his decision.** He may work alone, or with one or several classmates who are working on the same topic. The groups are a spontaneous and natural development, and the teacher goes from individual to individual or from group to group offering explanations, oral use of the foreign language, and encouragement. Other students may serve as tutors and within each group working together there is always one student who spontaneously assumes the leadership of the group and may serve as the "teacher." The students are urged to use the audio-visual equipment that is available in the classroom, such as the tape recorder or the phonograph. When the student has completed all the work in the packet of materials, he is ready to review the work and to be tested on it. He takes the test only when he feels that he is ready for it. If he is successful on the test, he moves ahead to the next packet. The student who has not been successful confers with the teacher and, based on the recommendation made by the teacher, reviews those elements in which there was some weakness and further reinforces these skills until he feels that he is ready to take the test again. Often the review is done directly with the teacher.

In the open classroom the teacher assumes a new role, that of the manager of the learning process. He is also the textbook or materials writer because it is the teacher who must prepare the overview for the course and the packets of carefully sequenced continuous progress materials. The teacher is also a diagnostician because in this new classroom milieu he can truly individualize the program for each student. That is, he can place proper emphasis on the skill or skills in which the student needs more help or in which a particular student's interest lies. Thus native speakers of the language can concentrate on reading and writing rather than on doing oral repetition drills for which they have no need and which may result in "turning them off" to the continuation of their language study.

The teacher in the open classroom is also a match-maker. He helps the students to find the right group in which to work, and he creates situations for peer teaching, thereby meeting the need of the weaker student and reaffirming the degree of mastery of the more advanced student. At varying times, the entire class is reassembled for large-group activities such as auditory comprehension or auditory dialogue practice.

Each packet contains a general objective (the aim of the lesson), and several specific objectives which show the student the development of the structure or reading lesson. Each objective is augmented and reinforced by an exercise or a variety of exercises that give the student immediate and direct application of that objective. The student takes the test on the objective when he feels he is ready for it. In the traditional teacher-oriented lesson, the teacher must, of necessity, spread his questions among all the students in the class. In the open classroom, on the other hand, *every* student is answering *every* question. Thus, the student is working harder and doing more in the open classroom. He is constantly aware of his responsibility in the learning process and he knows specifically and precisely what he must do to master the objective on which he is working.

Another means of individualizing instruction is the attenuation of a course of study from five to seven cycles for students who need a longer period of time in which to master the prescribed amount of work. At the end of the first phase of work, students are recommended by their teacher for placement in this course.

In order to offer our students an alternative educational experience and a means to put into practice the skills they have mastered during the phase, the last day of each cycle is called "Dewey Day." On this day the students participate in a large variety of activities that they have created and registered for in advance of the day. It is a procedure similar to registering for a particular workshop at a conference.

The foreign-language activities on Dewey Day have always shown the esprit de corps that exists between the teachers in the department and between the students and their teachers. Our first Dewey Day was an International Café in which the students created a French, Hebrew, Italian, and Spanish café. The food, menus, money, decorations, and entertainment were the work of the students who used the foreign language to a very great extent in their preparation and implementation of this situation.

The second Dewey Day simulated a 747 flight to Spain, France, Italy, and Israel. The students opened the movable doors between three classrooms to create the long expanse of the plane. They divided the plane into sections for each of the national airlines, decorating the chairs with crepe paper seat belts in the colors of the flags of the country. Safety instructions were given in the foreign languages and each "national airline" had its own promotion or happening. Prior to the day of the "flight" the students had to purchase their tickets in the resource center, and obtain a facsimile passport in the appropriate language. Highlights of the flight included foreign-language films, fashion shows, refreshments, and even dancing in the aisles.

Other Dewey Day activities in foreign languages have included a Casino in which students used the foreign language while playing various games, and a computer-dating operation in which students had to answer questions in the foreign language in order for the computer to match them with their "ideal mate." The last Dewey Day activity took the students out of the building to a restaurant where they were able to savour the traditional dishes of the various countries.

Another means of individualizing instruction in foreign languages at John Dewey High School is through offering foreign-language study to *all* students. Those students who would be denied foreign-language study in a traditional high school because of their reading score or because they have been labeled "less able" are offered a course of a conversational nature. This is a five-phase course that stresses the spoken language within the vocabulary topics of Level I. This course is, in essence, a readiness course because the student who successfully completes the five phases then goes into Level I. The conversation course gives him a basic foundation in the sound system and teaches him much of the vocabulary and idiomatic expressions of Level I. In Level I, he is then able to concentrate his efforts on mastering the skills of reading and writing.

The materials that we use in our Level I French and Spanish classes are from the Encyclopaedia Britannica series *JE PARLE FRANÇAIS* and *LA FAMILIA FERNANDEZ*. We selected these materials because they offer a multi-media approach to foreign-language instruction. The teachers have enjoyed working with the series and feel that the students have achieved better pronunciation and increased comprehension because of the technique that this series employs. The interest level of the students has increased considerably because of the multi-media approach of the film, filmstrip, and accompanying tapes.

John Dewey High School is a school that is committed to experimentation and change. We are constantly looking for new means to make the educational system and the learning process more exciting, interesting, and fruitful for our students. While we have the basic structure and philosophy of the school as our guiding spirit, it is the untiring dedication and willingness of our staff that enables us to implement such innovations in the individualizing of instruction as prescriptive teaching, the "Supportive DISK", the open classroom, independent study, team teaching, and special courses. Education must not be a joyless process, and it is our hope that the skills and knowledge that our students gain through attendance at John Dewey High School will prepare them for on-going education and acquisition of knowledge both in further formal education and in life itself. The role of foreign languages is a vital one, for it not only prepares our students with the ability to put syntactical and lexical forms together, but also enables them to speak with people from other parts of the ever shrinking globe with appreciation and respect for them and their culture. We want our students to view the world with a sense of wonder and abiding hope.

XI. Grading and Awarding Credit on a "Humane" and Sensible Basis: The Ithaca Experience

Mr. Will Robert Teetor is currently Foreign Language Coordinator for the Ithaca (N.Y.) School District. He is an experienced teacher and has been quite active in AATG circles, acting as Chairman of the National FLES Committee.

INTRODUCTION

Mr. Teetor relates his concerns about foreign-language education and explains his reactions to these concerns in the form of curricular development toward individualized instruction. He outlines how a more "humane" approach can lead to better performance and a lower dropout rate.

Ten years ago, foreign-language teachers were enjoying a renaissance but today the wailing is reaching crescendo proportions. The fantastic potential in the form of public money and support, electronic equipment, programmed materials, and the general enthusiasm for the audio-lingual method was not enough to prevent the present difficulties. In spite of our new methods and technology, we are inefficient and inhumane, when circa 50% of our beginning foreign-language pupils either drop out or fail by the end of the first year, because no allowance is made for individual differences and interests. It is necessary to build upon the skills and interests of the individual student, if a program involving the total school population is to be successful, particularly in a subject which is not required for graduation or entrance to some colleges.

Today, in spite of national insecurity in foreign-language teaching, there are schools in which language programs are not being threatened. That is so, in part, because of various attempts to provide a "humane" foreign language education relevant to each individual through "open-ended classroom instruction".[1]

Now we are talking about open-endedness, individualization or self-pacing, whatever you wish to call it, and actually there is little new about it in theory.

Good education and outstanding teachers have always stressed the individual in spite of the bureaucratic curbs and restrictions within our educational system. Outstanding teachers have been using "open-ended" techniques in foreign-language instruction and general education, be it the one-room schoolhouse in the 1930's or a self-contained class in the 1971 inner-city school. Many teachers are using various open-ended techniques successfully in the teaching of foreign language, but on the other hand, there are many aspects which are not widely used or known; therefore, our basic task is to disseminate information about those techniques which are being used successfully and to encourage experimentation with new and innovative aspects of open-endedness.

Foreign language programs must become as avant garde and innovative as possible in order to win the confidence of the public. Presently, administrators, guidance personnel, members of boards of education and the general public are beginning to take a very long and serious look at our educational establishment.

More than ever before, they are most willing to consider more humane educational programs, in order to expose the masses in our schools to a multi-sided curriculum, because many of today's political, social, and economic problems and pressures seem to be directly related to the schools and failures in the educational programs of the past.

Since a more positive climate does exist, those departments willing to consider humane changes within their programs are going to receive moral support and financial aid. Today, foreign-language teachers have an opportunity to begin to explore curricular changes; however, simply jumping on the bandwagon is not the answer, since we have seen far too many fads in the past. Teachers must consider programs carefully in relation to available resources, attitudes, and needs. Then and only then, a few pilot classes should be established in which these open-ended techniques are to be used for the purpose of demonstration and training. As these experimental classes develop, innovative tech-

---

[1] This writer used the term 'open-ended' in 1965 while developing an elementary school German program.

niques can be gradually introduced into the foreign-language program on a larger scale.

One important characteristic of the teacher in a developing individualized program will be willingness to re-evaluate seriously his role as a foreign-language educator. Since most of our foreign-language teacher training has stressed the teacher-oriented, lock-step classroom, it really does take a lot of time, contemplation, and energy to revamp present thinking and practice about (1) the role of the teacher-counselor, (2) the use of flexible timing, and (3) the development of open-ended techniques.

Some basic tenets follow:

A. Teacher-counselor role:
   1. The teacher-counselor plays a very important role in developing a positive learning atmosphere.
   2. The role of the teacher is to educate and not to fail.
   3. All pupils should experience success in foreign language.
   4. The classroom should not be teacher oriented, but pupil oriented.
   5. The foreign-language program should stress the pupils' talents and interests in a variety of course offerings.
   6. True education involves becoming a whole human being and is not achieved by merely learning subject matter.
   7. Education is not measured by the quality of regurgitation of semi-learned facts for a quiz or a test.

B. Flexible Timing:
   1. Predetermined time limits should play no role in a humane learning situation.
   2. Credit does not need to be associated with the calendar year nor awarded in whole units.
   3. A pupil-oriented non-failure grading system considers effort and knowledge and ignores the time element.
   4. Pupils do not all need the same time exposure, be it daily or weekly in foreign language.

C. Open-ended Techniques:
   1. Peer teachers and peer aides are a valuable asset in many learning situations.
   2. Individual, small-group, and large-group instruction should be developed within *any* classroom or learning area.

D. Team Teaching:
   1. Within large open spaces, team teaching allows for a variety of teaching and learning techniques during any period.

    2. Team teaching allows pupils to develop positive learning contacts with specific teachers.

    3. Team teaching allows teachers to utilize their particular skills in the learning area.

E. Flexible audio-lingual, audio-visual, and visual resource centers play a vital role in an open-ended foreign-language program.

The author will now discuss a few of the above points in greater detail, as they apply to programs in practice in Ithaca schools.

TEACHER-COUNSELOR ROLE

When a pupil is allowed to learn foreign language at a rate which is reasonable for his ability, this does not mean that he is allowed to set the pace without teacher counseling or guidance. The thought of allowing a pupil to flounder with all his new-found freedom is just as much folly as the assumption that we must make *all* the decisions for each pupil.

The pupil must play a very active role in establishing his program and, in turn, accept more responsibility for his own education. Education must no longer be a forced-feeding procedure which has "turned off" so many of our pupils. Our pupils must participate in the decision-making about their courses and course content.

More adequate teacher-pupil counseling must result in well developed written guidelines or just verbal agreements, depending upon the pupil, which allow the pupil to plot his future progress and work according to his foreign-language aptitude and interests. The teacher will become more aware of many non-language class problems which are barriers to positive and creative learning, problems that must be solved before any real constructive learning can occur. The "new" teacher-counselor role stresses the motto: "Education is to educate and not to fail!" It is sad to say, but that is not the motto that has been followed by teachers "educating" thousands of our pupils in this country. Pupils have been told, directly or indirectly, to quit warming seats in school and have been encouraged to become dropouts. What purpose has it served? None, but to destroy the egos, aspirations, hopes, and dreams of many young people.

As a teacher-counselor in humane education, the teacher now becomes an educator in the broadest interpretation, compelling him to counsel and to teach pupils of all abilities, aptitudes and interests with success and, in turn, build up their hopes and aspirations for the future. Each child can achieve some success and satisfaction in any subject if given the proper atmosphere, guidance, and motivation.

GRADING

Since grades have generally been awarded based on the ability to learn a specific amount of material within a certain period of time, most teachers have been faced with the dilemma of trying to be fair on an individual basis within our present grading system, but have found it very difficult and frequently impossible.

It is also a fallacy to assume that a class curve is natural and necessary. What purpose does the curve serve? It tells a lot of pupils that they are failures, but it should tell us, as educators, nothing more than the fact that the pupils were not able to learn the materials with A's or B's within the time allocated. Since aptitude is in part a function of both the time required to learn material and the amount of outside guidance needed, those pupils who are normally classified as C, D, or F students, should be provided with additional guidance and, if not more time, then less material to learn within a specified amount of time.

The present system allows pupils to flounder with a C or D "knowledge" and continue until they inevitably drop or fail. It is obviously educationally unwise to allow students to move on to the next chapter, unit, level, or learning packet with such a weak foundation, and in turn eventually experience that ego crushing episode: "Dan, I know you are really working your heart out and your effort and attitude are excellent, but I can't give you more than a 'D' (actually the D is usually a mercy F) this marking period because you failed a quiz or two and you did a poor job the last chapter test."

If Dan is really working at capacity and is not able to achieve more than a D, then there is something completely wrong with the marking system, the time allotment, the program's materials and expectations. The effect a poor or failing grade has upon an individual, emotionally and psychologically, is not only devastating, but so unnecessarily inhumane.

What do we achieve as educators? What effects do we have upon our pupils, their families, the community, and society? True, it is said, one must be prepared for the hard knocks of life. Yes, life is hell already for so many of our pupils, who come from bizarre homes and society-created little hells. Why make school an additional cross to bear?

A success philosophy for foreign-language teachers should be based upon two considerations: (1) humaneness, and (2) developing a positive attitude toward other cultures. In the eyes and the minds of his pupils, the foreign-language teacher, for good or bad, becomes an extension and representative of that language and culture. As this representative, he has the opportune chance to develop positive attitudes toward that culture and other cultures. This writer has observed that many pupils who fail in foreign-language study began to express hostility not only toward the foreign-language teacher but also toward that language and its culture. This hostility is often transmitted to parents and siblings, and in turn influences *their* attitudes toward that language and foreign-language instruction in general. Foreign-language education is more apt to be influenced in this manner than any other subject area in the curriculum because of its unique representation of a non-American aspect of life.

This writer believes that such hostility contributes to the present decline in foreign-language enrollment. What the total influence of this hostility might be upon attitudes toward other cultures, minorities, language groups, and nationalities, both nationally and internationally, is certainly open to conjecture.

Many below-average pupils I taught years ago in German still express favorable viewpoints toward language learning and the German culture. They and I were aware of their learning handicaps, but I was equally aware of their egos, feelings, aspirations, interest, and family backgrounds. Often German was the only course in which many received A's and B's, but those A's and B's were not merely "gifts". They were very individualized grades representing achievement in various areas of the German program depending upon interest, abilities, and aptitude. Their positive attitude toward German culture and me as a local extension of that culture, counteracted, among other influences, the negative American television stereotypes of German-speaking people.

CLASS RANK

In Ithaca, most pupils are able to achieve at least 80% comprehension in the passive-recognition area of foreign-language learning and must do so to proceed to the next level of work. Since the active-recall aspects of language learning are more difficult and demanding, it is not expected that every pupil will achieve the same minimum level as a prerequisite for moving ahead.

The teacher-counselor and each foreign-language pupil develop a program based on the pupil's aptitude and/or interests. Many pupils are only interested in the passive aspects of language learning, while others have a flair for the active. Our foreign-language programs must be so constructed that aptitude and interest are considered on an individual basis. We must not force every pupil into the same foreign-language mold, as most of us are doing today with very sad results.

If a school is required to provide class ranking for its seniors, the preponderance of A's and B's in a humane grading system does not create any problem. Ranking can be accomplished by granting the A's or B's over 1, 2, 3, 4 and 5 allowing each letter grade to be a weighted grade. The numbers are:

> 5 superior
> 4 outstanding
> 3 good
> 2 fair
> 1 passing

The numbers in the Ithaca language program represent the following performance rating for ranking purposes.[2]

	Passive Knowledge	Active Knowledge
5	90%	90%
4	80%	80%
3	80%	50%
2	80%	30%
1	80%	10%

FLEXIBILITY

Flexible scheduling does not necessarily mean a modular schedule. Flexible scheduling might include any one of a variety of learning time spans arranged to break up the lock-step schedule in any language class, traditional or non-traditional, either on a daily or weekly basis.

Every pupil does have an optimum time span in which he learns a certain amount of language. Some teaching and guidance by peers can help each pupil to arrange an individualized schedule during which he learns, teaches, and helps in any, rigid or non-rigid, classroom situation.

Sometimes a pupil can not take all the subjects he might wish to because of schedule conflicts. If a pupil has the choice of

---

[2] See table IV for a full explanation.

studying a foreign language two or three times a week or of dropping it, this writer urges strongly that a program and a schedule be developed in which the pupil study his foreign language on a *limited* basis. A pupil might also develop an over-exposure syndrome to learning a foreign language after a few years. For some, such over-exposure can lead to discontinuing further study of the language. In this case, again, a very flexible individualized schedule may be set up within an open-ended program which will allow the pupil a *minimum* contact with the language and thereby create a partial pause. Later he might wish to resume a full program. Programs such as *Pimsleur mini-courses* allow the very able language pupil to study two or more languages, if he wishes, in spite of a rather crowded schedule.

Open-endedness in any foreign-language program allows each student to develop as many schedules and programs as necessary to insure successful foreign-language learning.

Peer Teachers

Today, many educators consider peer teaching innovative, but it was one of the pillars of the one-room schoolhouse. Peer teaching was the only aid available to the teacher in a one-room school in the 1930's because the teacher did not have ditto machines, tape recorders, record players and records, slide projectors and any other modern learning aids at his disposal. A teacher could not have taught the 50 or more pupils in grades K-8, in spite of the 8-hour school day, if he had not used peer teachers in small-group, large-group, and individualized instruction. Some 4th graders taught 2nd graders; 8th graders taught 5th graders; some advanced 5th graders read with 6th and 7th graders, while less able 5th graders read with 3rd and 4th graders. It is frequently a rude awakening to see how well the peer teachers teach and, in turn, enjoy the learning through teaching. Often, a peer will do a better job with a fellow pupil than the teacher since he might be approaching the problem from a new standpoint.

Even in the most rigid traditional homogeneous or heterogeneous classroom, peer teaching can be used as the first step toward open-endedness. The pupil aides or peer teachers are able to operate various types of hardware, give dictations and quizzes, grade papers, put marks in the grade book, collect, sort, and file papers and learning packet materials, check translations, as well as teach and help peers in many other ways. As the program becomes more flexible, more advanced language pupils are able to volunteer as peer instructors in the beginning classes or at the junior high level during unscheduled time.

The teacher has more time to counsel, to work with either advanced materials, or to solve the more difficult learning problems within the classroom.

THE HUMAN ELEMENT

What are some of the great strengths of an open-ended program beyond the granting of humane grades and fractional credit, flexible scheduling and building upon a pupil's aptitudes and abilities? Such a program removes the unbearable pressure placed upon a pupil after a long absence on account of illness, personal tragedy or crisis. This pupil returns to our lock-step classes and suddenly faces five or six teachers who present a backlog of homework and materials for him to make up as quickly as possible. Frequently, his physical and emotional state is at a low ebb, and he has to face a bottomless pit of work, more so in a foreign language, where the aural-oral parts have to be presented after school by the teacher. With an open-ended program, the pupil can pick up at the spot where he stopped before his absence and proceed at a pace which does not overtax his strength.

Since quizzes and tests are taken whenever the pupil believes he is prepared, Ithaca teachers do not force a pupil to face a battery of tests on a day when he does not feel physically or emotionally well.

Also, an open-ended program allows a transfer pupil to find a spot in foreign language where he feels comfortable. The threat of being bored or overtaxed in the new school no longer is a big factor.

The human aspects of the teacher and the pupil are brought clearly into focus, and the program allows the teacher and pupil to work, to study, to learn and to be tested under optimum conditions which are frequently ignored or ridiculed in a typical lock-stepped class. Learning is such a complex phenomenon; we need to create the environment in which it can flourish, to make it an enjoyable activity which will not cease whenever the teacher's guiding hand is removed.

Too many of our pupils, upon leaving high school, either for college or other pursuits, are stunted in their ability to accept responsibility for their own daily learning or work activities because of teacher-oriented and parent-directed spoon feeding. The results of this public-school forced-feeding and lock-stepped learning are apparent in the college dropout and failure rates. Both dropout and failure are in part symptomatic of a pupil's inability to organize his time to establish and achieve goals, and to assume responsibility for independent work.

CREDIT

Class credit has always been treated almost as if it were a holy object that must be awarded in June, no matter if the pupil receives an A or a D. Frequently, the one credit is grossly unfair to the over-achiever who did much more than expected; at the same time, the one redit is much too generous in the case of the pupil who received a "mercy" F in the form of a D; however, the bureaucratic system gives the teacher no alternative but to pass him with a full credit or to fail him with no credit. The "teacher with a heart" then gives the D, as a mercy grade, which allows one full credit for questionable achievement. The credit actually represents nothing more than the ability of the pupil to hold out for a whole year, and therefore be rewarded for his tenacity.

Why must foreign-language credit be granted in whole units in June? There is no *logical* reason. Tue, it has been done in this manner for decades, and tradition can resist change for the sake of tradition. When a specific amount of work has a specific credit value ($\frac{1}{10}$, $\frac{1}{5}$, $\frac{1}{4}$, $\frac{1}{2}$, $\frac{3}{4}$, 1), why shouldn't the credit be awarded upon the successful completion of the work in various fractions? The granting of less than the whole credit per year allows the less able pupil to achieve *success* at a slower pace, and in a more relaxed atmosphere with much better grades; at the same time, it does not hinder the pupil who is progressing more *quickly*. The credit should be awarded at any time during the school year when the unit of work is completed. Some pupils might receive two credits within 10 months of school, while others just one credit or a fraction, and there are those who might actually need 12 or 15 months to complete the half credit. It is surely wiser to have a pupil receive a fraction of a credit and know the material at an acceptable level than be pushed on with D's until he is so swamped that he drops or fails. Under the present system, whenever he enters a college language class, he might have to start all over in spite of having earned three or four high-school credits based upon D work in public-school foreign-language study. Presently, the language proficiency represented by one credit varies so much from school to school, and even from teacher to teacher within a district, that it is becoming quite meaningless to college admissions.

If flexible granting of credit is established, the next step is a program which allows a pupil to earn as few as two or three credits or as many as possible (8 or 9) within a six-calendar-year program. In this manner, the credit truly represents language proficiency.

In Ithaca, we do award foreign-language credit in fractions, and have pupils earn less than an ½ credit in a calendar year, and others who have earned two credits within the 10 months. Whenever a pupil completes a fraction of a credit, his parents are notified by the teacher of his success, no matter when it occurs during the school year. The guidance office also receives a form which is placed in the pupil's folder. At the end of a school year, the total amount of credit for that year is printed out on the report card.

Many of our learning packets are based upon fractions of credit which allows the staff the flexibility and independence to negotiate an individual program for a pupil who is unable to study foreign language every day, to stress his specific interests in mini-courses, to lessen the effect of seniorities in the 12th grade, to allow a bilingual pupil to enjoy the language at his own level, and to offer mandated subjects (World History) in a foreign language.

TABLE I

AN OPEN-ENDED FOREIGN LANGUAGE PROGRAM
FROM GRADES 7–12 IN THE ITHACA CITY SCHOOL DISTRICT

Philosophy

If we are to pursue the philosophy that each student is to work at his own rate of speed in any given course, it seems that we have to avoid inequities in grading. It is conceivable that a student completing ½ credit can receive A's or B's and at the same time a student completing 1 or more credits of work in the same time can also receive A's or B's.

How to differentiate? Grades.

The use of the double grade appears on transcripts and report cards. All credit can be issued in fractions. The credit may be granted at any time when the required material has been completed, whether in June, September, January, April, etc.

The Foreign Language Class Titles for French, German, Russian, and Spanish.

The basic track materials are:

Beginning Foreign Language 1A & 1B & 2A & 2B

Book I = 2 credits (divided into four ½ credits)

Intermediate Foreign Language 3A & 3B & 4A & 4B

Book II = 2 credits (divided into four ½ credits)

Advanced Foreign Language 5A & 5B & 6A & 6B

Book III = 2 credits (divided into four ½ credits)

Independent Foreign Language 7A & 7B & 8A & 8B

Book IV = 2 credits (divided into four ½ credits)

Example of credit distribution in Beginning Foreign Language 1A, & 1B & 2A & 2B

Book I would be so divided:

     ½ credit is: Prereading through Chapter 5
     ½ credit is: Chapter 6 through Chapter 10
     ½ credit is: Chapter 11 through Chapter 15
     ½ credit is: Chapter 16 through Chapter 20

TABLE II. A CLASS OF BEGINNING FOREIGN LANGUAGE IN AN OPEN-ENDED PROGRAM: CLASS MAKE-UP: BEGINNERS AND CONTINUING PUPILS (1A, 1B, 2A, 2B)

Pupil	Status	Sept.	Oct.	Nov.	Dec.	Jan.	Feb.	Mar.	Apr.	May	June	Final Grades	Credit Earned	Total Credit to Date
Tom	Begin.	Preread.	Pre.	Pre.	1	2	2	2	3	4	5½	B/1	½	½
Paul	"	"	"	1	1	2	3	4	5	5½	6	B/2	½	½
Mike	"	"	"	1	2	3	4	4	5½	7	7	B/3	½	½
Mary	"	"	1	2	2	3	4	5½	7	8	10½	A/3	1	1
Peter	"	"	1	3	3	5½	7	8	10½	12	14	A/4	1	1
Ann	"	"	1	3	4	5½	6	7	9	11½	13	A/4	1	1
Richard	"	"	3	5½	7	9	12½	13	16½	17	20½	A/5	2	2
Jim	5½	5	6	6	7	7	8	8	9	9	10½	A/1	½	1
Paula	6½	6	6	7	7	7	8	8	9	10	10½	A/2	½	1
Roger	6½	6	6	7	7	7	8	8	8	10½	11	B/2	½	1
Ralph	7½	7	7	7	8	8	9	9	9	10	10½	B/2	½	1
Joan	7½	7	8	8	9	9	10	10½	11	12	13	A/3	½	1
Lisa	7½	8	9	10½	11	12	13	15½	16	17	18	A/4	1	1½
John	7½	8	9	10½	11	12	13	14	15½	16	19	B/4	1	1½
Joe	7½	8	9	10½	11	12	15½	16	17	19	20½	A/4	1½	2

NOTE: ½ indicates credit granted to student upon completion of required material or equivalent.
Definition of terms: Begin. — Beginning student of F. L.
Preread. — Pre.—Pre-reading period
1–2–3–4–, etc.—Chapters completed

TABLE III

A. Credit received at end of present teaching year	B. Status of Student in Sept. of Next Year
Beginners:	
Tom / Paul / Mike — each receives ½ credit for 5 chapters of Beginning F.L. 1A	Each enters Beginning F.L. 1B as a continuing pupil
Mary / Peter / Ann — would receive 1 credit for 10 chapters of Beg. F.L. 1A & 1B	Each enters Beginning F.L. 2A
Richard — would receive 2 credits for 20 chapters of Beginning F.L. 1A & 1B & 2A & 2B	enters Intermediate F.L. 3A
Continuing:	
Jim / Paula / Roger / Ralph / Joan — each had entered with ½ credit for 5 chapters of Beginning F.L. 1A during the previous year, and would receive at end of the present school year an additional ½ credit	each enters Beginning F.L. 2A
Lisa / John — each had entered with ½ credit for 5 chapters of Beg. F.L. 1A, and would receive at end of the present year an additional one credit	each continues Beginning F.L. 2B
Joe — entered with ½ credit for 5 chapters of Beginning F.L. 1A, and would receive at end of the present school year 1½ credits	enters Intermediate F.L. 3A

TABLE IV

Grades and Class Rank

The letter grade indicates the average of grades received on quizzes and tests of all types: written, oral, listening comprehension, etc. Each student can proceed at his own individual pace. He will not be allowed to go on to the next unit, chapter, etc. until achieving at least 80% on the passive aspects of the tests.

The number grade indicates progress within the average expected limits of the school year's curriculum, and the active-recall aspects of the four skills. If for Beginning Foreign Language 1, the anticipated average progress would be 9–10 chapters, equated by level 3, (or in cases of the students doing additional work in depth, level 4) anything below these required chapters is to be rated accordingly. Additional facts, such as illness, emotional problems, etc. might influence the progress number grade, at the teacher's discretion. The number grade allows for class rank to be assigned in the Senior year.

	Passive Knowledge	Active Knowledge
5 = Honors	90%	90%
4 = Outstanding	80	80
3 = Good	80	50
2 = Fair	80	30
1 = Passing	80	10

TABLE V. THE 7–12 FOREIGN LANGUAGE PROGRAM OF THE
ITHACA CITY SCHOOL DISTRICT, ITHACA, NEW YORK

Fr./Ger./Sp./Russ.		credit	Foreign Language Nomenclature and Codes. Code Numbers				Chapters of the basic textbooks	Mini or Immersion Courses
			Fr.	Ger.	Span.	Russ.		
Beginning	1A	½	416	432	448	460	First book 1–5	
	1B	½ ⎱ 1	415	431	447	459	6–10	or equivalent
	2A	½	414	430	446	458	11–15	
	2B	½ ⎱ 1	413	429	445	457	16–20	
Intermediate	3A	½	412	428	444	456	Second book 1– 3½	
	3B	½ ⎱ 1	411	427	443	455	3½– 7	or equivalent
	4A	½	410	426	442	454	8–10½	
	4B	½	409	425	441	453	10½–14	

		Third book					or equivalent
Advanced	5A	½	408	424	440	452	¼ of the book
	5B	1	407	423	439	451	" " "
	6A	½	406	422	438	450	" " "
	6B	½	405	421	437	449	" " "
		Fourth book					or equivalent
Independent	7A	½	404	420	436	—	¼ of the book
	7B	1	403	419	435	—	" " "
	8A	½	402	418	434	—	" " "
	8B	½	401	417	433	—	" " "

XII. A Selected Resource List for Individualizing Foreign-Language Instruction

INTRODUCTION

The foreign-language teacher or school administrator will want to have at his disposal many sources of information to help plan individualized programs. Parts of the following resource list will be of invaluable assistance, no matter how much equipment a school may be able to offer (or not offer) the foreign-language teacher or how much financial aid and professional assistance can be rendered; there is help here for almost any teacher or administrator in any school situation.

Dr. Donna Sutton offered special assistance in compiling the following bibliographical survey as she studied the current state of individualized foreign language in America. Her subject index should provide a ready key for the teacher who is planning an individualized program and needs to read about some of the related problems.

A SELECTED RESOURCE LIST FOR INDIVIDUALIZING FOREIGN LANGUAGE INSTRUCTION

1. Adams, Charles L. "Independence for Study." *Hispania,* L, 3, (September 1967), 483–87.
2. Adams, E. N. "A Proposed Computer-Controlled Language Laboratory." *Modern Language Teaching Papers from the 9th F.I.P.L.V. Congress.* Edited by Hans Jalling. London: Oxford University Press, n.d., 54–62.
3. Altman, Howard B. "Individualized Foreign Language Instruction: What Does It Mean?" *Foreign Language Annals* 4, iv (1971): 421–22, and *Individualization of*

Foreign Language Learning in America 2 (1971): 14–16. West Chester State College, West Chester, Pennsylvania.

4. _____, "Toward a Definition of Individualized Foreign Language Instruction." *American Foreign Language Teacher* 1, iii (1971): 12–13.

5. Adams, E. N.; Morrison, H. W.; Reddy, J. M. "Conversation with a Computer as a Technique of Language Instruction." *The Modern Language Journal*, LII, 1, (January 1968), 3–16.

6. _____, and Rosenbaum, Peter S. *Joint Feasibility Study in Computer-Assisted Foreign Language Instruction.* Final Report. Monterey, California: 1969.

7. Alexander, William M., and Hines, Vynce A. *Independent Study in Secondary Schools.* New York: Holt, Rinehart and Winston, Inc., 1967.

8. Allen, Dwight W., and Politzer, Robert L. *A Survey and Investigation of Foreign Language Instruction Under Conditions of Flexible Scheduling.* California: Stanford University Press, 1966.

9. _____, and _____, "Flexible Scheduling and Foreign Language Instruction: A Conference Report." *The Modern Language Journal*, LI, 5, (May 1967), 275–81.

10. Allen, John B., III. "Computational Contribution to Language Teaching." *Proceedings: Thirty-First Annual Foreign Language Conference at New York University.* Edited by Maurice Silver. New York: New York University School of Education, Department of Foreign Language and International Relations Education, 1965, 12–13.

11. Anderson, Theodore. "The Teacher of Modern Foreign Languages." *Foreign Language Teaching: An Anthology.* Edited by Joseph Mitchel. New York: The Macmillan Company, 1967, 253–79.

12- Andrews, Oliver, Jr., et al. "Innovative Foreign Language Programs," *Foreign Language Learning: Research and Development: An Assessment.* Edited by Thomas E. Bird. New York: MLA Materials Center, n.d., 10–44.

13. Archibeque, Joe D. "Utilizing the Advanced Spanish Student as a Classroom Tutor." *Hispania*, LIII, 1, (March 1970), 70–72.

14. Arnspiger, Robert H. "All He Is Capable of Becoming." *School and Community*, (November 1968), 19, 72–73.

15. Association for Supervision and Curriculum Development. *Individualizing Instruction, 1964 Yearbook.* Washington, D.C.: National Education Association, 1964.

16. Babinski, Richard. "The Application of Programmed Instruction to the Teaching of French Administration Correspondence in the Canadian Public Service." *The Modern Language Journal*, LII, 7, (November 1968), 416–19.

17. Baker, Robert L. "Flexible Scheduling for Individualized Instruction and Remedial Work in Russian." *Language Learning: The Individual and the Process.* Edited by Edward Najam and Carleton T. Hodge. *International Journal of American Linguistics*, XXXII, 1 Part II, 1966, 152–159.

18. Banathy, Bela H. "The Systems Approach." *The Modern Language Journal*, LI, 5, (May 1967), 281–89.

19. _____, and Jordan, Boris. "A Classroom Laboratory Instructional System (CLIS)." *Foreign Language Annals*, II, 4, (May 1969), 466–73.

20. Barrett, Kathleen. "Programmed Modules for Teaching French." *American Foreign Language Teacher*, 1, i (1970): 40–43.

21. Barrutia, Richard. "Computerized Foreign Language Instruction." *Hispania*, LIII, 3, (September 1970), 361–71.

22. _____. "Intrinsic Programming of Foreign Languages." *The Study of Foreign Languages.* Edited by Joseph S. Roucek. New York: Philosophical Library, 1968, 237–51.

23. _____. "The Past, Present, and Future of Language Laboratories." *Hispania*, L, 4, (December 1967), 888–99.

24. _____. "A Suggested Branch Program for Foreign Languages." *Hispania*, XLVII, 2, (May 1964), 342–50.

25. _____., et al. *Innovative Projects — Foreign Language Teaching.* Final Report. Irvine: University of California, 1969.

26. Bartley, Diana E. "The Importance of the Attitude Factor in Language Dropout: A Preliminary Investigation of Group and Sex Differences." *Foreign Language Annals*, III, 3, (March 1970), 383–93.

27. Bashour, Dora S. "The Use of New Media and Materials." *Proceedings: Thirty-First Annual Foreign Language Conference at New York University.* Edited by Maurice Silver. New York: New York University School of Edu-

cation, Department of Foreign Languages and International Relations Education, 1965, 14–15.

28. Beggs, David W. *Decatur-Lakeview High School: A Practical Application of the Trump Plan.* Englewood Cliffs, New Jersey: Prentice-Hall, Inc., 1964.

29. ———., and Buffie, Edward G. *Independent Study.* Bloomington: Indiana University Press, 1965.

30. Belasco, S. "Where is Programmed Language Instruction Most Effective?" Paper read at the Kentucky Foreign Language Conference, Lexington, Kentucky, April 1969.

31. Bell, Robert, and McDonald, Pearl S. *Experimental Use of Self-Instructional Courses in Russian and Spanish by Secondary School Students.* Arlington, County Public Schools, April 1964.

32. Berman, Mark L. *Experimental Explorations in Programmed Instruction and Objective Testing Measures, Report of the "Variables Influencing Behavior" Project, Paper 2.* Tempe: Arizona State University, 1966.

33. Bernardo, Leo U. "Individual Differences in the Junior High School." *Proceedings: Thirty-Second Annual Foreign Language Conference at New York University, 5 November 1966.* Edited by Marvin Wasserman. New York: NYU School of Education, Department of Foreign Languages and International Relations, 1966, 12–14.

34. "Better Teaching through Criterion-Referenced Testing." *Pi Reports*, 2, (1968), n.p.

35. Biemesderfer, William E. "Ohio State University's DATA-GRAM." *Audio-Visual Instruction*, XII, 458–59.

36. Bishop, Lloyd K. "Computerized Modular Scheduling: A Technical Breakthrough for More Flexible School Programs." *Kappa Delta Pi Record*, (October 1968), 17–19.

37. ———. *Individualizing Educational Systems.* New York: Harper & Row, 1971.

38. Bland, Merton and Evan R. Keislar. "A Self-Controlled Audio-Lingual Program for Children." *French Review*, XL, (1966), 266–76.

39. Bloom, Benjamin S. "Learning for Mastery." *UCLA Evaluation Comment*, I, 2 (Los Angeles, 1968), 1–12.

40. ———. *Stability and Change in Human Characteristics.* New York: John Wiley & Sons, 1964.

41. Birkmaier, Emma M., and Lange, Dale L. "What About the

Pennsylvania Studies?" *NEA Journal – Today's Education*, LVII, 7, 49, 51.

42. Bockman, John F. *Evaluation of a Project: Independent Foreign Language Study by Selected Eighth Graders at Townsend Junior High School Using Programmed Materials, March 3 to May 23, 1969.* Tucson, Arizona: Tucson Public Schools, 1969.

43. _____. "The Use of Behavioral Objectives in Foreign Language Teaching." *Forum*, XVI, 2, 3–10.

44. _____, and Gougher, Ronald L. "An Editorial Comment." *Foreign Language Annals* 4, iv (1971) 420, and *Individualization of Foreign Language Learning in America* 1 (1970): 1.

45. _____, and _____, "Editorial Comment." *Individualization of Foreign Language Learning in America* 2 (1971) 1.

46. Boggs, Roy A. "The Pennsylvania State University Foreign Language Survey: A Summary for Teachers of German." *Unterrichtspraxis*, II, 2, 140–43.

47. Bohning, Elizabeth. "Position Statement." *Individualization of Foreign Language Learning in America* 1 (1970) 3–4.

48. Bourque, Jane M. "Individualized Learning." *Accent on ACTFL* 1, iii (1971): 2–4.

49. Boyd-Bowman, Peter. "Self-Instruction in the 'Neglected' Languages: A Progress Report from Kalamazoo College." *The Modern Language Journal*, L, 1, 21–23.

50. *Britannica Review of Foreign Language Education, Volume 2.* 2, 1970. (The theme of Volume 2 is Individualization of Instruction. The following articles are included: "A Rationale for the Individualization and Personalization of Foreign Language Instruction," by Lorraine Strasheim; "Behavioral Objectives and Evaluation," by Florence Steiner; "Strategies of Instruction for Listening and Reading," by Gilbert Jarvis; "Strategies of Instruction for Speaking and Writing," by Alfred N. Smith; "Curricular for Individualized Instruction," by Jermaine Arendt; "Language Learning Laboratory," by W. Flint Smith; "Recent Developments in the Training and Certification of the Foreign Language Teacher," by Howard B. Altman and Louis Weiss; "Classics: The Teaching of Latin and Greek and Classical Humanities," by Gerald Erickson; "TESOL" by Bernard Spol-

sky; "Trends in Foreign Language Enrollments," by Richard I. Brod.)

51. Brown, B. Frank. *The Appropriate Placement School: A Sophisticated Nongraded Curriculum.* New York: Parker Publishing Co., 1965.

52. ———. *The Nongraded High School.* Englewood Cliffs, New Jersey: Prentice-Hall, 1963.

53. Bruner, Jerome. *Toward a Theory of Instruction.* Cambridge, Massachusetts: Harvard University Press, 1966.

54. Bryan, Quentin R. *Experimental Use of the University of Michigan Audio-Lingual Self-Instructional Course in Spoken Spanish.* Inglewood, California: Inglewood Unified School District, 1965.

55. Bull, William E. "Task Analysis and Foreign Language Teaching." *The Florida Foreign Language Reporter,* V, 1, (Winter 1966–67), 3–4.

56. Bung, Klaus. *Programmed Learning and the Language Laboratory.* London: Longmoc, 1967.

57. ———. "Towards Truly Programmed Language Laboratory Courses." *Audio-Visual Language Journal,* VII, 5–17.

58. Burroughs, Elaine L. *Experiments with the Applications of the Audio-Visual and Automatic Devices to the Teaching of French, Final Report.* Virginia: Hollins College, 1961.

59. Bush, Robert. "Redefining the Role of the Teacher." *Theory Into Practice,* VI, 5, (December 1967), 246–51.

60. ———., and Allen, Dwight W. *A New Design for High School Education.* New York: McGraw-Hill, 1964.

61. Capretz, Pierre J. "The Language Laboratory: A Relic of the Past or the Solution to the Future?" *National Association of Laboratory Directors Journal,* IV, 1, 32–42.

62. Cardwell, Richard A. "The Language Laboratory as a Teaching Machine, Equivocal Response and Psychological Choice: An Attempt at Resolution." *Audio-Visual Language Journal,* IV, (1967), 57–68.

63. Carroll, John B. "An Application of Psycholinguistics in Language Teaching: An Audio-Visual Instructional Device." *Report of the Twelfth Annual Round Table Meeting on Linguistics and Language Studies.* Edited by Michael Zarechnak. Washington, D. C.: Georgetown University Press, 1961.

64. _____. "Foreign Language Proficiency Levels Attained by Language Majors Near Graduation from College," *Foreign Language Annals*, I, 2, (December 1967), 131–51.

65. _____. "Individual Differences in Foreign Language Learning." *Proceedings: Thirty-Second Annual Foreign Language Conference at New York University*. Edited by Marvin Wasserman. New York: New York University School of Education, Division of Foreign Language and International Relations Education, 1966, 3–11.

66. _____. "Memorandum: On Needed Research in the Psycholinguistic and Applied Psycholinguistic Aspects of Language Teaching." *Foreign Language Annals*, I, 3, (March 1968), 236–38.

67. _____. "A Model for Research in Programmed Self-Instruction." *Advances in the Teaching of Modern Languages*. Edited by G. Mathieu. New York: Pergamon Press, 1966, 11–46.

68. _____. "A Model of School Learning." *Teachers College Record*, LXIV, (1963), 723–33.

69. _____. "Programmed Instruction and Student Ability." *Journal of Programmed Instruction*, III, 4, (1963), 4–7.

70. _____. "Programmed Instruction in Foreign Language Teaching." *Foreign Languages and the Schools:* A Book of Readings. Edited by Mildred Donoghue. Dubuque, Iowa: Wm. C. Brown Co., 1968, 367–80.

71. _____. *Programmed Self-Instruction in Mandarin Chinese: Observations of Student Progress with an Automated Audio-Visual Instructional Device*. Wellesley, Mass.: Language Testing Fund, 1963.

72. _____. "Psychological Aspects of Programmed Learning in Foreign Languages." *Proceedings of the Seminar on Programmed Learning*. Edited by Theodore H. Mueller. New York: Appleton-Century-Crofts, 63–73.

73. _____. "What Does the Pennsylvania Foreign Language Research Project Tell Us?" *Foreign Language Annals*, III, 2, (December 1969), 214–36.

74. _____., and Graham, Leonard. *The Effectiveness of Programmed Grafdrils in Teaching the Arabic Writing System*. Cambridge, Mass.: Harvard Graduate School of Education, 1963.

75. Caso, Adolph. "Language Programs Are Shortchanging Our Students." *Education Digest*, XXXIV, 9, 48–49.

76. Castle, Pat., and Jay, Charles, et al. *An Explanation of "Levels" of Competence in Foreign Language Learning: French, Levels I, II, III.* Springfield: Illinois State Office of the Superintendent of Public Instruction, 1969.

77. _____., and _____., et al. *An Explanation of "Levels" of Competence in Foreign Language Learning: German, Levels I, II, III.* Springfield: Illinois State Office of the Superintendent of Public Instruction, 1969.

78. _____., and _____., et al. *An Explanation of "Levels" of Competence in Foreign Language Learning: Spanish, Levels I, II, III.* Springfield: Illinois State Office of the Superintendent of Public Instruction, 1969.

79. Cavanaugh, Peter, and Jones, Clive, comps. *Yearbook of Educational and Instructional Technology 1969–70. Incorporating Programmes in Print.* Englewood Cliffs, New Jersey: Educational Technology Publication 1969.

80. Chastain, Kenneth D. "A Methodological Study Comparing the Audio-Lingual Habit Theory and the Cognitive Code-Learning Theory — A Continuation." *The Modern Language Journal*, LIV, 4, (April 1970), 257–66.

81. Cioffari, Vincenzo. "Developments in Modern Language Teaching — A Summary and Forecast." *The DFL Bulletin*, VII, 1, 11–13.

82. Ciotti, Marianne C. "A Conceptual Framework for Small-Groups Instruction in High School." *Foreign Language Annals*, III, 1 (October 1969), 75–89.

83. Clark, John L. D. "The Pennsylvania Project and the 'Audio-Lingual vs Traditional' Question." *The Modern Language Journal*, LIII, 6, (October 1969), 388–96.

84. Clark, William H. "First-Year College German through Programmed Instruction." *Die Unterrichtspraxis*, II, 2, 58–60.

85. _____. *Using Programmed Foreign Language Courses in Secondary Schools with Specially Trained Teachers. Final Report.* Rochester, N. Y.: University of Rochester, 1968.

86. _____. "Using Programmed Language Courses in College." *Proceedings of the Seminar of Programmed Learning.* Edited by Theodore H. Mueller. New York: Appleton-Century-Crofts, 11–17.

87. _____., and Clark, Margaret G. "Achievement in Elementary German under Programmed and Conventional In-

struction: A Preliminary Study." *The Modern Language Journal*, L, 2, (February 1966), 97–100.

88. Congreve, W. J. "Independent Learning." *North Central Association Quarterly*, XL, (1965), 222–28.

89. Curl, David H. "The Self-Instructional Audio-Visual Laboratory." *Educational Screen and Audiovisual Guide*, XLVI, 5, 24–25.

90. Deterline, William A. "Programmed Instruction as a Process." *Educational Screen and Audiovisual Guide*, XLVI, 4, 18, 21.

91. Dodge, James W. "Machine-aided Language Learning." *Britannica Review of Foreign Language Education, Volume 1.* Edited by Emma Birkmaier. Chicago: Encyclopaedia Britannica, 1968, 311–41.

92. Duda, Mary J. "A Critical Analysis of Individually Prescribed Instruction." *Educational Technology*, 10, XII (1970): 47–51.

93. Dusel, John P. *Implications Regarding Possible Elimination of Foreign Language Requirements in Colleges and Universities.* Sacramento, California: State Department of Education, 1969.

94. ———. *State Surveys and Language Dropouts.* Sacramento, California: State Department of Education, 1969. (Mimeographed.)

95. ———. "Why the Foreign Language Dropouts?" *Foreign Language Newsletter of Northern California*, XIV, (May), 5–7.

96. ———., et al. *An Interim Report on a Continuous Progress Program in French I and Spanish I.* Abington, Pa.: High School North Campus, 1967.

97. ———., and Torres, Edgardo E., et al. *Foreign Language Dropouts: Problems and Solutions.* Sacramento, California, California State Department of Education, 1970.

98. Egerton, Mills F., Jr., ed. *Sight and Sound: The Sensible and Sensitive Use of Audio-Visual Aids.* New York: MLA Materials Center, 1969.

99. Eisenhardt, Catheryn, "Individualization of Instruction." *Elementary English* 47, III (1971) 341–45.

100. Epstein, Henry. "Teaching the Slow Learner." *Proceedings: Thirty-Second Annual Foreign Language Conference. 5 November 1966.* Edited by Marvin Wasserman. New York: NYU School of Education, Division

of Foreign Languages and International Relations Education, 1966.

101. Estarellas, Juan. "The Self-Instructional Foreign Language Program at Florida Atlantic University." *Hispania*, LIII, 3, (September 1970), 371–85.

102. Etten, John F. "Flexible Programming in Student Teacher Preparation." *Peabody Journal of Education*, XLVI, 215–17.

103. Eurich, Alvin C. "Man and Media in Higher Education." *Educational Broadcasting Review*, II, 4, 3–9.

104. Everett, Aaron B. *Syllabus for French I, II, III*, New Program. Green Springs, Ohio: Antioch College, 1966.

105. _____. "Try Custom French: We Did." *Tennessee Teacher*, (January 1968), 13–17.

106. Fearing, Percy. "Non-graded Foreign Language Classes." *Foreign Language Annals*, II, 3, (March 1969), 343–47.

107. Feldhusen, John F. and Szabo, Michael. "A Review of Developments in Computer Assisted Instruction." *Educational Technology*, IX, 4, 32–39.

108. Fiks, A. I. "Foreign Language Programmed Materials, 1966." *The Modern Language Journal*, LI, 1, (January 1967), 7–14.

109. _____. *Foreign Language Programmed Materials: 1968.* New York: MLA Materials Center, 1968.

110. Flaugher, Ronald L. and Spencer, Richard E. "College Foreign Language Placement and the Intervening Years Problem." *The Modern Language Journal*, LI, 7, (November 1967), 394–98.

111. Fleury, Dale F. "Independent Study: Foreign Language Seminars." *National Association of Secondary School Principals Bulletin*, CCCXXXVIII, 53, 90–99.

112. Forrester, Jean. *Teaching Without Lecturing.* London: Oxford University Press, 1968.

113. Forsdale, Louis and Dykstra, Gerald. "An Experimental Method of Teaching Foreign Languages by Means of 8mm Sound Film in Cartridge-Loading Projects." *Language Learning*, XIII, (1963), 5–10.

114. Fowler, Betty. "Criterion Referenced Testing." Paper presented at the ACTFL meeting on Friday, November 28, 1969, New Orleans, Louisiana.

115. Freudenstein, Reinhold. "Informationen aus dem Computer. Ein neues Zentrum für den Fremdsprachenunterricht." *Die Neueren Sprachen*, XVIII, 187–88.

116. Gagné, Robert M. *The Conditions of Learning.* New York: Holt, Rinehart and Winston, 1965.

117. Garvey, Catherine J., et al. *A Report of the Developmental Testing of Self-Instructional French Program.* Washington, D. C.: Center for Appllied Linguistics, 1967.

118. Garvin, Paul L., ed. *Natural Language and the Computer.* New York: McGraw-Hill, 1963.

119. Gauthier, A. "Programmed Material for Secondary Schools." *International Conference: Modern Foreign Language Teaching.* Papers and Reports of Groups and Committees. Reprints, Part 1. Berlin: Pädagogische Arbeitsstelle und Sekretäriat, Pädagogisches Zentrum, 1964, 77–82.

120. Ghan, Zoe Ann, and Rickel, Kathryn. "The Liberated Dialogue, or 'Let the Kids Make Up Their Own Dialogues'." *Foreign Language Annals,* III, 2 (December 1969), 237–40.

121. Gillespie, Myrtle E., and Black, John W. "A Self-Administered Technique in Auditory Training." *Speech Monographs,* XXXIV, (1967), 98–102.

122. Gladstone, Igor M. "Modified Scheduling and Foreign Languages." *Bulletin of the National Association of Secondary School Principals,* L, (November 1966), 121–27.

123. Glatthorn, Allan A., et al. *An Interim Report on a Continuous Progress Program in French I and Spanish I.* Abington, Pa.: Abington High School North Campus, May 1967.

124. Goodlad, J. I., and Anderson, R. H. *The Nongraded Elementary School.* New York: Harcourt, Brace & World, 1959.

125. Gougher, Ronald L. "Learning of German at Optimum Rates." *Unterrichtspraxis* 3, I (1970): 142–43.

126. _____. "Motivation and Materials for Learning German at Optimum Rates." *The Bulletin of the Pennsylvania State Modern Language Association,* 48, II (1970): 5–7.

127. Griffith, Janet D. *Results of the Survey of the Use of Programmed Foreign Language Instruction in American Universities and Colleges.* Clearinghouse Report. Washington, D. C.: Center for Applied Linguistics, 1965.

128. Grittner, Frank M. "A Critical Re-Examination of Methods

and Materials." *The Modern Language Journal.* LIII, 7, (November 1969), 467–77.

129. _____. "Maintaining Foreign Language Skills for the Advanced-Course Dropout." *Foreign Language Annals*, 2, (December 1968), 205–11.

130. _____, ed. "What's New in Wisconsin: Innovative Foreign Language Programs." *Voice of the Wisconsin Foreign Language Teacher*, VII, 1, (1967), 33–42.

131. Grobman, Hulda. *Evaluation Activities of Curriculum Projects: A Starting Point.* Chicago: Rand McNally. (AERA Curr. Eval. Monograph 2.)

132. Hardy, Mary H. "Dare to Individualize Instruction, or Dare Not?" *Kappa Delta Pi Record*, (April 1969), 99–102.

133. Hayes, Alfred S. "Programmed Learning: A New Look at Learning." *Current Issues in Language Teaching.* Edited by William F. Bottiglia. New York: MLA Materials Center, 1957, 19–60.

134. Henning, William A. "Discrimination Training and Self-Evaluation in the Teaching of Pronunciation." *International Review of Applied Linguistics*, IV, (1966), 7–17.

135. Hernick, Michael, and Kennedy, Dora. "Grouping Foreign Language Students." *NEA Journal — Today's Education*, LVIII, 1, 38–39.

136. _____, and _____. "Multi-Level Grouping of Students in the Modern Foreign Language Program." *Foreign Language Annals*, II, 2, (December 1968), 200–04.

137. Hibbard, Allen. "Modular Scheduling and Modern Foreign Languages." Paper presented at Spring Conference of North Dakota Foreign Language Association, Spring, 1969.

138. Hill, L. A. "Programmed Instruction and the Class Teacher." *English Language Teaching*, XXI, (1966), 45–50.

139. Hively, Louise F. *A Report on the Use of Color Coded Cards to Promote Individualized Instruction in Spanish Classes.* Abington, Pa.: Abington High School North Campus, June 1967.

140. Hocking, Elton. "Technology in Foreign Language Teaching." *The Modern Language Journal*, LVI, 2 (February, 1970), 79–91.

141. Hoelzel, Alfred. "Foreign Language Objectives: Myths and Realities." *Bay State Foreign Language Bulletin*, XIII, 2, (1968), 2–6.

142. Hooker, David M. "Chinese Language Instruction in Tuc-

son Public Schools: Independent Study." *Arizona Foreign Language Teachers Forum.* (January 1968), n.p.

143. Hoye, Almon. "Can Flexible Schedules Affect Foreign Language Enrollments?" *Minnesota Foreign Language Bulletin,* VI, 1–5.

144. _____. "Let's Do Our Thing—Flexibly." *The Modern Language Journal,* LIII, 7, (November 1969), 481–84. (Part of the *Proceedings* of the Central States Conference on the Teaching of Foreign Languages, Milwaukee, Wisc., April 10–12, 1969.)

145. Hsu, Kai-yu. "A Guest Editorial: The Teacher as an Architect of Learning." *Foreign Language Annals,* III, 3, (March 1970), 377–92.

146. Huseboe, Arthur R. "The Class-Made Film as a Motivation to Writing." *Robert Frost's Chicken Feathers and Other Lectures from the 1968 Augustana College NDEA English Institute.* Edited by Arthur R. Huseboe, Sioux Falls, South Dakota: Augustana College Monographs, Ser. 1, 1968.

147. Jakobovits, Leon A. *Foreign Language Learning: A Psycholinguistic Analysis of the Issues.* Rowley, Mass.: Newbury House, 1970.

148. _____. "Research Findings and Foreign Language Requirements in Colleges and Universities." *Foreign Language Annals,* II, 4, (May 1969), 436–56.

149. Johansen, Patricia A. "The Development and Field Testing of a Self-Instructional French Program." *Linguistic Reporter,* XI, 6, 13–27.

150. Jones, Betty M. "Language Laboratory Audio Program: High School: Advanced French." *Newsletter for Teaching Language Through Literature,* VII, 1, (1967), 54–57: VII, 2, (1968), 24–28.

151. Kant, Julia Gibson. "Foreign Language Offerings and Enrollments in Public Secondary Schools, Fall 1968." *Foreign Language Annals,* III, 3, (March 1970), 400–76.

152. Keller, Fred S. "Good-bye Teacher—." *Journal of Applied Behavior Analysis.* I (1968) 79–89.

153. Kersten, Caesar S. and Ott, Vesperella E. "How Relevant Is Your Foreign Language Program?" *The Modern Language Journal,* LIV, 1, (January 1970), 9–13.

154. King, Paul E. "Man and Machines in Language Teaching." *Foreign Languages and the Schools: A Book of Read-*

ings. Edited by Mildred R. Donoghue. Dubuque, Iowa: Wm. C. Brown Company, 1968, 327–34.

155. Klin, George. "Our Unrealistic Language Program." *The French Review* XLII, 722–27.

156. LaLeike, Fred. *Individualized Foreign Language Program.* West Bend, Wisconsin: Joint School District No. 1, 1970. [Mimeograph Copy]

157. Lane, Harlan L., and Buiten, Roger. "A Self-Instructional Device for Conditioning Accurate Prosody." *Trends in Language Teaching.* Edited by Albert Valdman. New York: McGraw-Hill, 1966, 159–74.

158. _____, and Schneider, Bruce. "Methods for Self-Shaping Echoic Behavior." *The Modern Language Journal,* XLVII, 1, (January 1963), 54–60.

159. Langer, Phillip. "Minicourse: Theory and Strategy." *Educational Technology,* IX, 9, 54–59.

160. Leib, J. W. et al. "Teaching Machines and Programmed Instruction: Areas of Application." *Psychological Bulletin,* LXVII, (1967), 12–26.

161. Levy, Stephen L. "Adapting Foreign Language to New Educational Designs." *Language Federation Bulletin* 22, II (1971): 5–7. [The New York State Federation of Foreign Language Teachers]

162. Lipton, Gladys. "Changes in Objectives and Curriculum." *Proceedings: Thirty-First Annual Foreign Language Conference at New York University.* Edited by Maurice Silver. New York: NYU School of Education, Department of Foreign Languages and International Relations Education, 1965, 17–18.

163. Lloyd, Donald J. "An Outside Look at Programmed Learning in Foreign Languages." Paper read at the Kentucky Foreign Language Conference, Lexington, Kentucky, 23 April 1969.

164. Logan, Gerald E. "A Totally Individualized High School Program." *Individualization of Foreign Language Learning in America* I (1970), 8–9.

165. _____. *German Curriculum.* Morgan Hill, California: Morgan Hill Unified School District, 1969.

166. Lorenz, Jean M. *A Continuous Progress Program of Individualized Instruction in the Study of Spanish.* Charles Town, West Virginia: Charles Town Senior High School, 1970.

167. McClennan, Robert. "How Do We Allow Students To Learn at Optimum Rates?" _American Foreign Language Teacher_ 1, III, (1970): 8–11.

168. McDonald, Pearl S. and Bell, Robert. _Experimental Use of Self-Instructional Courses in Russian and Spanish by Secondary School Students._ Arlington, Virginia: Arlington County Public Schools, 1963.

169. Macias, Cenobio. "Programmed Learning as Used in the Tacoma Public Schools." _Proceedings: Pacific Northwest Conference on Foreign Languages, Twentieth Annual Meeting, April 11–12, 1969._ Victoria, B. C.: University of Victoria, 1969, 160–62.

170. Mackey, William F. "Trends and Research in Methods and Materials." _Languages and the Young School Child._ London: Oxford University Press, n.d., 69–83.

171. McKimm, Lester W., ed. "Recent Trends in Foreign Language Teaching Techniques and Materials." _Audio-Visual Instructor,_ (May 1968).

172. McLennan, Robert. _Handbook for German Students._ Mountain View California: Mountain View High School District, n.d.

173. Marie, Sister Eileen S. C. "The Very Successful Student in Foreign Language Instruction." _Proceedings: Thirty-Second Annual Foreign Language Conference at New York University._ Edited by Marvin Wasserman. New York: New York University School of Education, Department of Foreign Languages and International Relations Education, 1966, 15–17.

174. Martin, Willard. "A Report on a Discussion Conference on the West Chester, Pennsylvania Study." _National Association of Laboratory Directors Journal,_ IV, 1 64–67.

175. Marty, Fernand L. _Programming a Basic Foreign Language Course: Prospects for Self-Instruction._ Roanoke, Virginia: Hollins College, 1962.

176. Masciantonio, Rudolph. "Innovative Classical Programs in the School District of Philadelphia." _Foreign Language Annals,_ III, 4, (May 1970), 592–95.

177. Mathieu, Gustave. "Automated Language Instruction: A New Deal for Student and Teacher." _Automated Teaching Bulletin,_ I, (1959), 5–9.

178. _____. _Recommendations of the Learnings Which Should Occur in the Language Lab and in the Classroom._

New York: Modern Language Association of America, 1960.

179. Mayer, Edgar. "Programmed Instruction and Its Application to the Teaching of Russian." *Methods of Teaching Russian.* Edited by Ludmilla B. Turkevich. Princeton: Van Nostrand, 1967, 129–43.

180. Meiden, Walter and Murphy, Joseph A. "The Use of the Language Laboratory to Teach the Reading Lesson." *The Modern Language Journal,* LII, 1, (January 1968), 23–25.

181. Moore, J. William. "Instructional Design: After Behavioral Objectives What?" *Educational Technology,* IX, 9, 45–48.

182. Morrison, H. W. and Adams, E. N. "Pilot Study of a CAI Laboratory in German." *The Modern Language Journal,* LII, 5, (May 1968), 279–87.

183. Morton, F. Rand. "Four Major Problem Areas in Programmed Instruction for Modern Language Learning." *Proceedings of the Seminar on Programmed Learning.* Edited by Theodore H. Mueller. New York: Appleton-Century-Crofts, n.d., 18–37.

184. ———. "The Teaching Machine and the Teaching of Languages: A Report on Tomorrow." *Foreign Languages and the Schools: A Book of Readings.* Edited by Mildred Donoghue. Dubuque, Iowa: Wm. C. Brown Co., 1968, 358–67.

185. ———. *Terminal Revision of the ALLP-II Programmed Spanish Language Course.* St. Charles, Missouri: Lindenwood College for Women, 1967.

186. ———, and Mueller, Theodore H. *Audio-Lingual Language Programming, Revised French Program, Parts 1–2.* Akron, Ohio: University of Akron, 1965.

187. Mueller, Theodore. *Analysis of the Results Obtained with Basic French—A Programmed Course Academic Year 1968–69 and Comparison with a Traditional Audio-Lingual Course.* Lexington, Kentucky: University of Kentucky, 1969.

188. ———. "Foreign Language Learning and the Teaching Machine." *Clearing House,* XL, (1966), 345–52.

189. ———. "The Language Instructor and Teaching Machines." *Bulletin of the Pennsylvania State Modern Language Association,* XLV, 1, (1966), 13–17.

190. ———. "Programmed Instruction: Help for the Linguistically

'Underprivileged'." *The Modern Language Journal,* LII, 2, (February 1968), 79–84.

191. ――――., and Harris, Robert. "The Effect of an Audio-Lingual Program on Drop-Out Rate." *The Modern Language Journal,* L, 3, (March 1966), 133–37.

192. ――――., and ――――. "First Year College French Through an Audio-Lingual Program." *International Review of Applied Linguistics in Language Teaching,* IV, 1, (March 1966), 19–38.

193. ――――., and Miedzielski, Henri. "Programmed Instruction in Teacher Retraining (NDEA Institutes)." *The Modern Language Journal,* L, 2, (February 1966), 92–97.

194. Murphy, Dennis, F. M. S. "The Average Learner." *Proceedings: Thirty-Second Annual Foreign Language Conference, 5 November 1966.* Edited by Marvin Wasserman. New York: New York University School of Education, Division of Foreign Languages and International Relations, 1966.

195. Myers, M. Keith. *Audio-Lingual Self-Instruction in Russian.* Earlham College Self-Instruction Project. A Report of Developmental Research, 1962.

196. Naber, Richard H. "Dial Access Information Retrieval Systems, Circa 1967." *Illinois Journal of Education,* LIX, 3, (1968), 51–54.

197. National Association of Secondary School Principals. *Seeking Improved Learning Opportunities, Fourth Report on Staff Utilization Studies.* Washington, D. C.: National Education Association, 1961.

198. Neagley, Ross L., and Evans, N. Dean. *Handbook for Effective Curriculum Development.* Englewood Cliffs, New Jersey: Prentice-Hall, 1967.

199. Newmark, Gerald. *A Design for a Program in Beginning Foreign Language Study Utilizing Motion Pictures and Programmed Learning Materials: A Working Draft.* Santa Monica, California: Systems Development Corporation, 1961.

200. ――――. "Making Foreign Language Instruction More Responsive to Individual Differences in Learners." International Conference: *Modern Foreign Language Teaching.* Papers and Reports of Groups and Committees. Part 1. Berlin: Pädagogische Arbeitsstelle und Sekretäriat, Pädagogisches Zentrum, 1964, 451–83.

201. ———. *A New Design for Teaching Foreign Languages Using Dramatic Motion Pictures and Programmed Learning Materials.* Santa Monica, California: Systems Development Corporation, 1962.

202. ———. *Research in Programmed Instruction in Spanish with Seventh-Grade Students.* Santa Monica, California: Systems Development Corporation, 1964.

203. ———. *Advances in the Teaching of Modern Languages,* II. Edited by Gustave Mathieu. New York: Pergamon, 1966, 47–75.

204. Olmo, Guillermo del. "Individualized Instruction: The Classroom Situation." *Language Learning: The Individual and the Process.* Edward W. Najam and Carleton T. Hodge, eds. *International Journal of American Linguistics,* XXXII, 1, part II, (1966).

205. ———. "Professional and Pragmatic Perspectives on the Audiolingual Approach: Introduction and Review." *Foreign Language Annals,* II, 1, (October 1968), 19–29.

206. Ornstein, Jacob. "Programmed Instruction and Educational Technology in the Language Field: Boon or Failure?" *The Modern Language Journal,* LII, 7, (November 1968), 401–10.

207. Otto, Frank. "The Teacher in the Pennsylvania Project." *The Modern Language Journal,* LIII, 6, (October 1969), 411–20.

208. ———. "Individualizing Instruction Through Team Teaching." *Hispania,* LI, 3, (September 1968), 473–75.

209. Palmer, L. R. "The Module: A New Mode for Gaining Flexibility." *Minnesota Foreign Language Bulletin,* VII, 2, 1–6.

210. Papalia, Anthony. "A Study of Attrition in Foreign Language Enrollments in Four Suburban Public Schools." *Foreign Language Annals,* IV, 1, (October 1970), 62–67.

211. Parent, P. Paul. "Minimizing Dropouts in the Foreign Language Program." *The Modern Language Journal,* LII, 4, (April 1968), 189–91.

212. Perren, G. E. "Testing Spoken Language: Some Unsolved Problems." *Language Testing Symposium.* London: Oxford University Press, 1968, 107–16.

213. Phelps, Florence, and Barrett, Martin, et al. *The McCluer Plan.* St. Louis County, Missouri: Ferguson-Florissant R-2 School District, 1968.

214. Pillet, Roger A. "Individualizing Instruction: Implication for FLES." *The Detroit Foreign Language Bulletin.* V, 2, 3–4.

215. Pimsleur, Paul. "Modern Greek Self-Taught: First Step to a National Library." *Advances in the Teaching of Modern Languages.* Edited by Gustave Mathieu. New York: Pergamon Press, 1966, 138–46.

216. _____., ed. *Final Report on the Seminar on Foreign Language Teacher Preparation for College Teachers.* Conducted at DePauw University, June 15–July 10, 1964. Green Castle, Indiana: DePauw University Press, 1964.

217. _____. and Struth, Johann F. "Knowing Your Students in Advance." *The Modern Language Journal*, LIII, 2, (February 1969), 85–87.

218. Politzer, Robert L. "Flexible Scheduling and the Foreign Language Curriculum." *The Detroit Foreign Language Bulletin*, VII, 1, (1967), 6–8.

219. _____. *Performance Criteria for the Foreign Language Teacher.* Stanford, California: Stanford University, 1967.

220. _____. "Toward Individualization of Instruction." *The Modern Language Journal*, 55 (1971): 207–12.

221. Popham, W. James, et al. *Instructional Objectives.* Chicago: Rand McNally. (AERA Curriculum Evaluation Monograph 3.)

222. Porter, Douglas. "A Report on Instructional Devices in Foreign Language Teaching." *Teaching Machines and Programmed Learning: A Source Book.* Edited by Arthur A. Lumsdaine and Robert Glaser. Washington, D. C.: Department of Audio-Visual Instruction, National Education Association, 1960, 186–205.

223. Postlethwait, J., Novak, J., Murray, E. *An Integrated Experience Approach to Learning, with Emphasis on Independent Study.* Minneapolis, Minnesota: Burgess Publishing Co., 1964.

224. Poulter, Virgil L. "Computer-Assisted Laboratory Testing." *The Modern Language Journal*, LIII, 8, (December 1969), 561–64.

225. Rallo, John A. "A Cooperative French Program: A New Approach." *Foreign Language Annals*, II, 4, (May 1969), 474–80.

226. Raubinger, Frederick M. and Harold G. Row. *The Individ-*

ual and Education—Some Contemporary Issues. New York: Macmillan, 1968.

227. Reed, E. A. and Cronkovic, J. K. *The Continuous Progress Plan.* Provo, Utah: Brigham Young University, 1963.

228. Regan, Timothy F. "Linguistics and Programmed Instruction." *Linguistic Reporter,* IX, 2, 1–2.

229. Reichmann, Eberhard. "Motivation and Direction of Reading Assignments of the Intermediate Level." *The Modern Language Journal,* L, 5, (May 1966), 256–60.

230. Reinert, Harry. "Student Attitudes Toward Foreign Language—No Sale!" *The Modern Language Journal,* LIV, 2, (February 1970), 107–12.

231. _____. "Creative Lab Usage." *National Association of Language Laboratory Directors Journal,* IV, 1, 57–63.

232. _____. "Practical Guide to Individualization." *The Modern Language Journal,* 55 (1971): 156–63.

233. *Report of the First Annual Conference: Flexible Scheduling and Foreign Language Teaching.* Bridgeport, Conn.: Proceedings of the Annual Conference of the Department of Foreign Languages. University of Bridgeport, December 1968.

234. Rivers, Wilga. *The Psychologist and the Foreign Language Teacher.* Chicago: The University of Chicago Press, 1964.

235. Rocklyn, Eugene H. "The Evaluation of Self-Instructional Foreign Language Courses." Paper read at the National Society for Programmed Instruction, San Antonio, Texas, 1 April 1964.

236. Roeming, Robert F. "Critique of the Pennsylvania Project Preface." *The Modern Language Journal,* LIII, 6, (October 1969), 386–87.

237. Rogers, Adrienne. "Motivation: The Forgotten Word." *The French Review,* XXXIX (1966), 906–09.

238. Rogers, Carl R. "Learning to be Free." *Readings in Curriculum.* Edited by Haas and Wiles. Boston: Allyn and Bacon, Inc., 1966, 203–219.

239. _____. "What Psychology Has to Offer to Teacher Education." Paper prepared for Conference on Educational Foundations, Cornell University, April 1964.

240. Rose, Theodore E. "Recorder's Report." *The Modern Language Journal,* LIII, 7, (November 1969), 477–80.

241. Rosenbaum, Peter S. "The Computer as a Learning En-

vironment for Foreign Language Instruction." *Foreign Language Annals*, II, 4, (May 1969), 457–69.

242. Ruplin, Ferdinand A. and Russell, John R. "Towards Structured Foreign Language Study: An Integrated German Course." *The Modern Language Journal*, LIV, 3, (March 1970), 174–83.

243. _____. and _____. "A Type of Computer-Assisted Instruction." *German Quarterly*, XLI, (January 1968), 84–88.

244. Saltzman, Irving J. "Techniques Used in the Construction of a Completely Self-Instructional, One Semester, Modern College Course in Russian." *Structural Drill and the Language Laboratory*. Edited by Francis W. Gravit and Albert Valdman. *International Journal of Applied Linguistics*, XXIX, 2, Part III, 1963, 167–76.

245. _____. *The Construction and Evaluation of a Self-Instructional Program in Russian*. Bloomington, Indiana: Indiana University Foundation, 1964.

246. Sandstrom, Eleanor L., and Paul Pimsleur, et al. "Foreign Languages for All Students?" *Northeast Conference Reports of the Working Committees*. Menasha, Wisconsin: George Banta Company, 1970.

247. Scanlon, Robert G. "Individually Prescribed Instruction: A System of Individualized Instruction." *Educational Technology*, 10, XII (1970): 44–46.

248. Scanlon, Richard T. "Computer-Assisted Instruction in Foreign Languages at the University of Illinois." *Foreign Language Annals* 4, IV (1971): 423, and *Individualization of Foreign Language Learning in America* 2 (1971): 6–7.

249. Scherer, George A. "Programming Second Language Reading." *Advances in the Teaching of Modern Languages*, II. Edited by Gustave Mathieu. New York: Pergamon, 1966, 108–129.

250. _____. "Toward More Effective Individualized Learning." *Language Learning: The Individual and the Process*. Edited by Edward W. Najam and Carleton T. Hodge. International Journal of American Linguistics, XXXII, 1 Part II, (1966), 139–45.

251. Schrag, Peter. "Kids, Computers, and Corporations." *Saturday Review*. L, (20 May), 78–80, 93–96.

252. Schramm, Wilbur. "Implications of the New Technology for Language Teaching." *Language Development*.

Selected Papers from a Ford Foundation Conference on the State of the Art. New York: Ford Foundation, 41–56.

253. *Selected Bibliography in Programmed Instruction.* Washington, D. C.: ERIC Clearinghouse for Linguistics, 1967.

254. *Sequential Programs in Foreign Language for a Restructured Curriculum, Grades 7–12.* Cleveland, Ohio: Educational Research Council of Greater Cleveland, 1967.

255. Sharp, Mary D. "Programmed Instruction in Large School Systems." *Automated Education Letter, II*, 2, 3–9.

256. Shepherd, W. Everitt. "An Experiment in Individualized Advanced French." *Foreign Language Annals, III*, 3, (March 1970), 394–99.

257. Skinner, B. F. "The Science of Learning and the Art of Teaching." *Harvard Educational Review*, XXIV, 1954, 86–97.

258. _____. *The Technology of Teaching.* New York: Appleton-Century-Crofts, 1958. (See especially: "Teaching Machines," 29–58; "The Technology of Teaching," 59–93; "The Motivation of the Student," 145–68, "The Creative Student." 169–84.)

259. Smith, M. Daniel. *New Instruction Media, Self-Instruction, Guided Instruction and the Role of the Teacher.* Richmond, Indiana: Earlham College, 1962.

260. Smith, Philip D. Jr. "An Assessment of Three Foreign Language Teaching Strategies and Three Language Laboratory Systems." *The French Review*, XLIII, 289–304.

261. _____. *A Comparison Study of the Effectiveness of the Traditional and Audiolingual Approaches to Foreign Language Instruction Utilizing Laboratory Equipment, Supplementary Report.* West Chester, Pennsylvania: West Chester State College, 1969.

262. _____. "Peace Corps Materials Project Toward Individualization." *Individualization of Foreign Language Learning in America* 1 (1970): 10–11.

263. _____. "Text Adoption Policies Inhibit Individualization." *Individualization of Foreign Language Learning in America* 2 (1971): 13–14.

264. _____. "The Pennsylvania Foreign Language Research

Project: Teacher Proficiency and Class Achievement in Two Modern Languages." *Foreign Language Annals*, III, 2, (December 1969), 194–207.

265. Smith, R. W. "Closed Circuit Television in the Language Laboratory." London: *Times Educational Supplement.* XXIV, (January), 280–81.

266. Spokak, Ruth. *Selected Bibliography in Programmed Instruction*. Washington, D. C.: Center for Applied Linguistics, 1966.

267. Spokoini, Hilier. "New Directions in the Teaching of Common Western Languages: Programmed Instruction." *Proceedings: Thirty-Third Annual Foreign Language Conference at New York University*. New York: New York University School of Education, Department of Foreign Languages and International Relations Education, 1967, 22–27.

268. Spolsky, Bernard. "Computer-Based Instruction and the Criteria for Pedagogical Grammars." *Language Learning*, XV, (1965), 137–45.

269. _____. "A Psycholinguistic Critique of Programmed Foreign Language Instruction." *International Review of Applied Linguistics*, IV, (1966), 119–29.

270. _____. "Some Problems of Computer-Based Instruction." *Behavioral Science*, XI, (1966), 487–97.

271. Steiner, Florence. "Performance Objectives in the Teaching of Foreign Languages." *Foreign Language Annals*, III, 4, (May 1970), 579–91.

272. _____. "Teacher-Made Tests: Vital in the Foreign Language Classroom." *Toward Excellence in Foreign Language Education*. Springfield, Illinois: Office of the Superintendent of Public Instruction, State of Illinois, 1968, 75–78.

273. Stevens, Thomas C. and Diaz-Carnot, Paul. *Adaptation of the ALLP-II Spanish Self-Instructional Program (F. Rand Morton, University of Michigan) to Class Sessions. Final Report*. Canton, Missouri: Culver-Stockton College, 1968.

274. Strasheim, Lorraine A. "The Anvil or the Hammer: A Guest Editorial." *Foreign Language Annals*, IV, 1, (October 1970), 48–56.

275. _____. "Where From Here?" *The Modern Language Journal*, LIII, 7, (November 1969), 493–97.

276. Suppes, P. "The Uses of Computers in Education." *Scientific American*, 1966, 215–216.
277. _____, and Crothers, Edward. *Application of Mathematical Learning Theory and Linguistics to Second-Language Learning, with Particular Reference to Russian. Final Report.* Stanford, California: Stanford University Institute for Mathematical Studies, 1967.
278. _____, and _____. *Some Remarks on Stimulus-Response Theories of Language Learning. Psychology Series, Technical Report Number 97.* Stanford, California: Stanford University Institute for Mathematical Studies, 1966.
279. _____, and Jerman, Max. "Computer-Assisted Instruction at Stanford." *Educational Technology*, IX, 1, 22–24.
280. Sweet, Waldo E. "The Continued Development of the Structural Approach." *Didaskalos*, II, 2, 1967.
281. _____. "Integrating Other Media with Programmed Instruction." *The Modern Language Journal*, LII, 7, (November 1968), 420–23.
282. Terwilliger, Ronald I. "Multi-Grade Proficiency Grouping for Foreign Language Instruction." *The Modern Language Journal*, LIV, 5, (May 1970), 331–33.
283. Thompson, William. "An Experiment in Audio-Visual Language Teaching." *Didaskalos*, I, 2, (1964), 78–80.
284. Trump, J. Lloyd. "A Look Ahead in Secondary Education." *Readings in Curriculum.* Edited by Haas and Wiles. Boston: Allyn and Bacon, Inc., 1966.
285. _____, and Baynham, Dorsey. Focus on Change. *Guide to Better Schools.* Chicago: Rand McNally Co., 1961.
286. Turner, Ronald C. *CARLOS: Computer-Assisted Instruction in Spanish at Dartmouth College.* Hanover, New Hampshire: Dartmouth College, 1968.
287. Unwin, Derick, and John Leedham, eds. *Aspects of Educational Technology.* London: Methuen, 1967.
288. Valdman, Albert. "Breaking the Lockstep." *Structural Drill and the Language Laboratory.* Edited by Francis W. Gravit and Albert Valdman. *International Journal of American Linguistics*, XXIX, 2, Part III, (1963), 147–59.
289. _____. "Further Notes on the 'Programmability' of Foreign Language Materials." *Proceedings of the Seminar on Programmed Learning.* Edited by Theodore H. Mueller. New York: Appleton-Century-Crofts, n.d., 74–77.

290. _____. "Programmed Instruction and Foreign Language Learning: Problems and Prospects." *Florida Foreign Language Reporter*, V, 1, 13–15; 18–20.

291. _____. "Problems in the Definition of Learning Steps in Programmed Foreign Language Materials." *Proceedings of the Seminar on Programmed Learning*. Edited by Theodore H. Mueller. New York: Appleton-Century-Crofts, n.d., 50–62.

292. _____. "Programmed Instruction and Foreign Language Learning, Problems and Prospects." *The Florida Foreign Language Reporter*, n.d.

293. _____. "Programmed Instruction and Foreign Language Teaching." *Trends in Language Teaching*. Edited by Albert Valdman. New York: McGraw-Hill, 1966, 133–58.

294. _____. "Programmed Instruction Versus Guided Learning in Foreign Language Acquisition." Paper read at the Modern Language Sectional Meeting of the Indiana State Teachers Association Conference on Instruction, Indianapolis, 27 October 1967.

295. _____. "Toward a Better Implementation of the Audio-Lingual Approach." *The Modern Language Journal*, LIV, 5, (May 1970), 309–19.

296. _____. "Toward Self-Instruction in Foreign Language Learning." *International Review of American Linguistics*, II, (1964), 1–36.

297. _____. *Advances in the Teaching of Modern Languages*, *II*. Edited by Gustave Mathieu. New York: Pergamon, 1966, 76–107.

298. Valette, Rebecca M. "Laboratory Quizzes: A Means of Increasing Laboratory Effectiveness." *Foreign Language Annals*, I, 1, (October 1967), 45–48.

299. _____. "The Pennsylvania Project, Its Conclusions and Its Implications." *The Modern Language Journal*, LIII, 6, (October 1969), 396–404.

300. _____. "Some Conclusions to Be Drawn from the Pennsylvania Study." *National Association of Language Laboratory Directors Newsletter*, III, 3, 17–19.

301. Van Abbe, Derek M. "A New Type of Language Degree Course – A Report from the United Kingdom." *Foreign Language Annals*, I, 4, (May 1968), 301–311.

302. Veatch, Jeannette. "Individualizing." in _Individualization of Instruction: A Teaching Strategy._ Edited by Virgil M. Howes. New York: Macmillan, 1970.

303. Wienecke, D. _Independent Study: Pathescope Berlitz German Language Series._ Minneapolis, Minnesota: Minneapolis Public Schools, n.d.

304. Wiley, W. Deane, and Bishop, Lloyd K. _The Flexibly Scheduled High School._ West Nyack, New York: Parker, 1968.

305. Wood, Fred H. "The McCluer Plan: An Innovative Non-Graded Foreign Language Program." _The Modern Language Journal,_ LIV, 3, (March 1970), 184–87.

306. Zeldner, Max. "The Foreign Language Dropouts." _The Modern Language Journal,_ L, 5, (May 1966), 275–80.

307. Zemensky, Edith von, and Block, A. H. "An Examination of Use of a Program of Instruction in German." _National Society for Programmed Instruction,_ VI, 1, 4–5, 9.

308. Zinn, Karl L. "Computer Assistance for Instruction." _Automated Education Letter,_ I, 7, 4–15.

SUBJECT INDEX